From the Inside Out

How to Create and Survive a Culture of Change

Tom Payne

SECOND EDITION

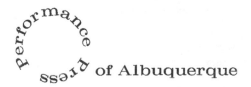
Performance Press of Albuquerque

From the Inside Out:

How to Create and Survive a Culture of Change

Publisher's Cataloging in Publication Data

Payne, Thomas E.
From the Inside Out: How to Create and Survive a Culture of Change
  Second Edition

Includes index.
1. Organizational Change. 2. Middle Managers. 3. Organizational Development.
4. Corporate Culture.

HD58.8.P63   1993   658.406 90-91985
ISBN 0-9627085-2-6 $14.95 Soft Cover

COVER DESIGN: Hodge Podge Lodge, Dave Payne
ILLUSTRATIONS: Liesl Meyers

First Printing 1991
Second Printing 1992
Third Printing 1993, revised

Printed in the United States of America

Lasting improvement does not take place by pronounce-
ment or official programs. Change takes place slowly
inside each of us and by choices we think through in quiet
wakeful moments.... Culture is changed not so much by
carefully planned, dramatic and visible events as by focusing on our own actions in the small barely noticed day to
day activities of our work....

...It (culture) changes from the inside out.... When we each
focus on the present and become living examples of the
organization we wish to create, the larger change process
has begun.

The Empowered Manager
Peter Block

DEDICATION

To the authors of the author:
my parents, Bill and Ardele Payne.
Thanks for always being there.

To those authored by the author:
my children, Tom and Dave.
Thanks for making your mother and me proud.

To my best friend:
without whose encouragement, support,
patience and editorial skill
there would have been no book,
my wife, Jean.
Thanks for everything.

I love you.

TABLE OF CONTENTS

SECTION ONE

Back To The Basics

SECTION TWO

Reducing The Roadblocks To Effective Change

SECTION THREE

Practical Steps To Implementing Change

ACKNOWLEDGMENT

We would like to thank employees of the following organizations for their assistance in providing input to this book and for understanding **"the future ain't what it used to be."**

Abbott Labs, Ameritech Information Systems, Ameritech Services, Anixter Brothers, AT&T, BDM International, Blount Construction, Canadian Pacific Forest Products, City of Albuquerque, Conductive Containers Inc., Doyle Associates, Federal Sign, General Electric Aircraft Engines, Gundersen Clinic Ltd., Illinois Bell, Lincoln National Life, Metro Dade Police Department, Miles Canada Inc., Miles Labs—Consumer Health Division, Miles Labs—Diagnostic Division, Monsanto Chemical Company, Norbertine Fathers & Brothers, Pecos River Learning Center, Plains Electric Generation & Transmission Co-operative Inc., Public Service Company of New Mexico, Sandia National Laboratories, United States Army, United States Navy, US West, Wace USA, Wisconsin Bell Inc.

Specifically we would like to thank the following individuals who took time from their busy and ever changing schedules to share with us all ——

Lt. Comdr. Rick Albrecht, Stan Bazant, Ray Becker, Chuck Burgner, Bernie Browe, Jim Burke, Brig. Gen. Bill Campbell, Jan Fincher, Barney Fleming, Sara Foley, Jack Friedheim, Dennis Gonka, Rev. Eugene Gries O. Praem, Carl Grlvner, Lou Hoffman, Ed Hughes, Barbara Jones, Erick Koshner, Susan Krasny, Berweida Learson, Jim Lentz, John Mayer, Jeanette Mitchell, Fred Randazzo, Susan Samson, Knute Sorenson, Tom Talty, Nancy Teutsch, Erich Zwolfer.

With special thanks to:

Manuscript Readers and Contributors — Candice Boneff, Sam Bulmer, Jerry Coombs, Tony Cos, Jim Doyle, Joe Fanning, Joelle Hertel, Joe Hogan, Rita Koridek, Kris Oleson M.D., Bob Oleson, Bill Payne, Rita Sheehan, Joan Ward Ph.D., Carol Windland, Harry Windland.

Editing Assistance — Jacqueline Hertel and Pauline Taylor.

AUTHOR'S NOTE

Working in today's ever-changing environment can be a serious business, but it does not have to be quite as serious as some folks make it. In my travels through the United States and Canada, I have discovered a rather alarming fact. MANY OF TODAY'S WORKERS ARE NOT HAVING FUN! I do not mean "lamp-shade-on-the-head" type of fun. I mean just finding enjoyment in going to work each day. Consider the names given to the beginning and the ending of the traditional work week, "Blue Monday" and "Thank God, it's Friday." Does that say something? If we can't have some fun doing what we do for a living, what is the point?

From the Inside Out deals with some serious personal and professional issues. The issues may be serious, but hard as I tried, I was not always able to stay "grave and somber" while dealing with them. Humor is used to illustrate various points (At least humor was intended.), and stories are used to lighten heavy subjects. I admit to having "fun" writing this book. To the more solemnly inclined reader, my apologies; to the rest — enjoy!

INTRODUCTION: IT IS NOT ABOUT HEARING IT;
IT IS ABOUT GETTING IT.

QUESTION:

"What do you think workers need to succeed in a changing business environment?"

ANSWERS: (listed in random order):

1) Flexibility.
2) To be innovative.
3) To have access to and be able to process information.
4) Ability to identify and solve problems.
5) To remain market focused.
6) The self-confidence to be risk takers.
7) To be self-sufficient, in charge of their own careers.
8) To be participative.
9) To recognize who the customer is and what his or her needs are.
10) To remain open to new ways of doing things.
11) Ability to manage untraditional work forces.
12) To be trainers.
13) To do less paper work.
14) Guts.
15) A positive attitude.
16) Patience.
17) To establish specific parameters for subordinates so

they can act on their own.

18) To work well as team members.
19) To maintain good life balance.
20) To be learners.
21) To maintain a sense of fulfillment when moving horizontally in the organization.
22) To be effective multi-directional communicators.
23) To understand and share group values.
24) Coping skills.
25) To garner support from all levels in the organization.
26) To make transition from directing to coaching style.
27) To be able to build and sustain relationships.
28) To empower and to be empowered or to request empowerment if it is not offered.
29) To understand the marketplace.
30) On-going technical skills.
31) To provide employee career development.
32) To meet stress head on.
33) To possess project management skills.
34) To recognize and reward desired behaviors.
35) To be able to value differences of thought.
36) Know how to manage the process.
37) Knowledge of the business they are in.
38) To develop a framework for decision making.
39) A real awareness that the game is changing.
40) To be enthusiastic.
41) Basic leader/manager skills.
42) To give trust and be trustworthy.
43) Clear sense of role responsibility.
44) To understand the various levels of job maturity of other team members.
45) Ability to receive and follow directions.
46) Planning capabilities.
47) Willingness to change selves to adapt to the values of the new work force.
48) To feel, and to be, accountable.

49) To prevent problems before they occur.
50) Total quality orientation.
51) To be demanding of self and others.
5?) To understand, live and communicate the vision.

DOES THIS LIST MAKE YOU WANT TO ASK FOR A RAISE OR WHAT?

●●●

These answers, taken from an informal survey of over 200 people from thirty-one organizations, were similar, whether the question was asked of A T & T, an order of Catholic priests, the U.S. Army or a company with ten employees. While the answers may have been similar from one organization to another, the fifty-two answers (Hereafter known as "The Fifty-Two.") were not a surprise to anyone who has ever tried to accomplish work with and through others. **Workers know what needs to be done to be effective in the changing environment**. But knowing and doing are two different things.

There is a story of a farmer who when asked to subscribe to some "How-To-Farm" manuals declined, saying, "Not interested, I already farm half as well as I know how." How many of us are physically and mentally able to do a better job than we are currently doing in implementing the above fifty-two answers? Could we be more flexible, more innovative, develop more patience, and/or be more enthusiastic if we chose to be?

If we know what needs to be done to be effective in a changing environment and we have the ability to do it, why are we not even more effective than we are? **Something or someone is getting in the way**. Something or someone is preventing us from "farming" as well as we know how. The

13

desire may be very strong to look outside of ourselves for a place to lay the blame for ineffective change implementation, but the fact is **when we look outside of ourselves, we are looking in the wrong direction.**

Change will occur from the inside out. When a person chooses to change, change will happen. When a person chooses to improve personal performance of one or all of "The Fifty-Two," performance will be improved.

●●●

From the Inside Out is written for all of us in a changing world. Its purpose is to put us, as individuals working within an organizational structure regardless of our titles: more in charge and more in control of the results in our personal and professional lives, more in control in an environment that may appear out of control, more in control for the benefit of both the individual and the organization.

Some concepts may appear too basic and simple to be effective. Consider this — **The truth is simple!** As the Spanish philosopher, Ortega, said, "**Life is fired at you point blank.**" The concepts and the "how tos" stated are not complicated and they do not have to be complicated to be effective. They just have to be acknowledged, accepted and implemented. **It is not about hearing it; it is about getting it.**

If there is any room for improvement for any of us, maybe that is because we still have not quite "got" it. In a speech, Dr. Ken Blanchard, of *One Minute Manager* fame, told the audience that he would answer his critics, who complained that he was not telling people anything they did not know, by saying, "**I won't teach anything new until we begin doing the old stuff.**" In one sentence Ken Blanchard has summed up the philosophy of *From the Inside Out.*

Intellectual grasping of what is discussed in these pages will not be a problem for any reader, but we may all spend the rest of our lives trying to merely scratch the surface of these concepts on the emotional level.

●●●

In Section One we will get back to the basics. We will look at the Results Model, that is how the results in both our business and personal lives, including our reactions to change, get the way they are. Section One deals with the inside (what a person believes) and the outside (how a person behaves).

Section Two will take us through four major roadblocks to the effective management of change (Pain of Change, Fear of Failure, Fear of Loss of Security and Self-Doubt) and how to reduce their negative impact on the individual and the organization. Section Two addresses what goes on inside the person which will determine the individual's degree of success.

Section Three covers how the inside can manifest itself on the outside. It is for all of the "how to" fans and will provide practical steps on how a person can implement change in the work unit more effectively and efficiently.

●●●

When conducting the research for *From the Inside Out,* an encouraging note was observed. All the organizations with whom we met were, at the very least, discussing what systems to put in place to support the behaviors required to operate satisfactorily in a culture of business change.

The majority had already established the environment and the structure necessary for organizational evolution.

Suggesting the optimal way to organize for the changing business environment is not the purpose of this book. That is best left to those more involved in the finer points of organizational design. We are here to get more basic than organizational structure. We are here to discuss what makes up the organization, whatever the structure, and that is the people. **Years may pass after implementing the physical structure before people buy the change internally and manifest it externally.** *From the Inside Out* is about reducing time required for employee "buy in." Change begins with people and flows from the inside out. If they don't buy, it don't fly!

For example, an organization establishes a self-directed work team concept, and provides the environment and reward structure necessary to make it work. This team will work only to the degree that the individuals, making up the team, want a self-directed work team and are willing to give of their discretionary, nonmeasurable selves to make this creation of upper management work. **The correct structural design, staffed with employees willing and able to give all they have to give, is the combination in which one finds the true potential of an organization.**

American business, despite some negative press, is putting the required structures in place — that is the easy part. *From the Inside Out* is about the hard part, freeing individuals from self-imposed limitations to "farm as well as they know how" in both business and personal life. **Freeing individual potential will dramatically increase the power of the organization to accommodate change.**

● ● ●

Time to get comfortable; put your feet up, adjust the light, choose to take control of change, and let's go.

SECTION ONE

Back to the Basics

MAYBE SO, MAYBE NOT: CHOOSING OUR RESULTS

There was a peasant farmer who owned a beautiful horse desired by others. One day it disappeared. When all the villagers remarked on his bad luck, he calmly replied, "Maybe so, Maybe not." A few days later the horse returned, leading a herd of fine wild horses. A week later, his only son was thrown and crippled while training the horses. When the villagers again remarked on his bad luck, he calmly replied, "Maybe so, Maybe not." Within a week, a frivolous war was declared by the emperor and all young men, save the farmer's son, were forced into battle and none returned.

"Our organization is realigning, reorganizing, downsizing and rightsizing. I'm really stressed out. Don't I have a right to be?" MAYBE SO, MAYBE NOT!

The choice as to what to believe concerning various organizational restructuring is up to each individual involved in the affected organizations. **The success of the new structure depends to a significant degree upon the internal choices made by the people who will make up the new environment and the external behaviors exhibited by them.**

● ● ●

In this section we will examine the Results Model — how we get what we got. The Results Model will demonstrate that the outcomes in our lives occur because of the choices we have made or have not made.

A classic experiment in psychology clearly points out the power of choices. Scientists placed two groups of people in separate rooms and supplied them with puzzles and exercises in proofreading to complete. Into each room loud distracting noises were piped. That in itself was not much of an experiment because most people go through the same thing every day at the home and in the office. The psychologists, recognizing that fact and possibly justifying their hefty grant, spiced the scenario by including a noise cutoff switch in one of the rooms. The group in the room with the cutoff switch solved five times the number of puzzles and made significantly fewer proofreading errors than the group placed in the "switchless" room.

The results of the experiment may seem obvious and not worth a grade of "C" in Psychology 101, but the "Ah ha!" was that the switch was <u>never</u> used. Those folks felt in control just knowing they had a choice! **When we are in control, we are more effective**.

The Results Model will show more than one opportunity to choose (to be in control). When it comes to results, we have two opportunities to choose, and therefore two opportunities to be in control.

●●●

In this section the Results Model will be built and each element of the model — Roaults, Behaviors, Feelings, Beliefs and Events — will be discussed.

Below is the Results Model. Let's start on the next page with results and continue through the remainder of the model.

Results Model:

Events + Beliefs = Feelings
⇩
Behaviors
⇩
RESULTS

RESULTS: MAKING THEM HAPPEN OR LETTING THEM HAPPEN

A few years ago in the *Toronto Sun*, a humorous article quoted input to insurance forms provided by those poor unfortunate souls whose vehicles occupied the same space at the same time as another object. When asked to describe their accidents, they said:

- "The other car collided with mine without giving warning of its intention."

- "A truck backed through my windshield into my wife's face."

- "A pedestrian hit me and went under my car."

- "An invisible car came out of nowhere, struck my car and vanished."

And my all time favorite —

- "The telephone pole was approaching fast. I was attempting to swerve out of its path when it struck my front end."

These responses were good for a chuckle at the time, but these are people who have gone through a certain amount of trauma, embarrassment, wasted time and potential financial loss. And they have not learned a thing! The people who responded felt no responsibility for what had happened to them. If they were in no way responsible for what has happened, how are these drivers ever going to be able to prevent a similar event from happening again?

Are these people just going to go out into the world each day and hope against hope that another telephone pole does not come along and strike them again in their already sore front ends?

●●●

Recently while conducting workshops with one of the major corporations in North America, an interesting phenomenon occurred. Nonmanagement employees were asked who in their organization was keeping them from doing their jobs the way they believed the jobs should be done. Their answers were not a surprise. They each said, "My boss." In the sessions with the first level supervisors, the same question received the same answer. Would you care to venture a guess as to whom the executive vice president pointed?

TIME OUT! It is time people began to take responsibility for the results in their business and personal lives. **If they do not take responsibility for results being the way they are, then they will not be inclined to take responsibility for changing those results.** This passive position leaves personal results in the hands of whomever and whatever — all the telephone poles of life.

In his book, *The Empowered Manager*, Peter Block makes a similar point when he says:

In twenty years of conducting training workshops in organizations, I have never once had the right people in the room. The first question a group of middle managers ask is, "Has top management been through this workshop?" If the answer is no, the group replies, "How do you expect us to try these things if they are not supported and rewarded by our bosses?" If top management has been through the workshop, the reply is "Well, they may have been through the workshop, but they are not really using the skills." If top management is going through the workshop, they declare, "This is fine for us, but the group that really needs it is the next level down."

I completely agree with Peter Block. If we could only get all of "them" in one workshop, we could clear up all known corporate woes. **Are you waiting for someone else to change your results**?

Responsibility comes from the Latin, "respondere," to respond. If people do not take responsibility, they will not "respond." They will, by definition, do the opposite of respond, which also comes from the Latin, "sitontheirassuntilsomethingelsehappens."

Each individual is responsible for personal results. If people choose to do nothing, they can no more alter their results than a person could become more aware of good literature by sitting on a stack of the classics.

●●●

Chapter 2 ——— Results

What some people will do to avoid taking responsibility is amazing. For example, consider the newspaper articles about individuals suing a tobacco company for lung or heart disease suffered by the smoker. One story graphically pointing out an individual's desire not to take responsibility was about the woman who was suing a liquor company for the illness of her newborn child even though she drank at a clip well above the national average all during her pregnancy! (The image of an employee of the liquor company standing over this woman, with her hands tied behind her back and the employee force feeding her bourbon, burns brightly in my mind!)

Are we the kinds of persons who make things happen or do we let things happen? Whether we do something, or do not do something, results in our lives are going to occur. (Interesting question: How many results in our lives do we consciously plan to have occur?)

Of course, there are those who feel self-responsibility puts too much pressure on them to do something about the results. They would rather say events outside of themselves cause their results. There are also those who are frustrated politicians who would say, "Some of my results I am responsible for. Some come from external sources." Fair enough, but realize for every result a person disclaims any responsibility, she is also giving up power for altering that result to the external source.

A person who is going to be "in charge," and "in control" must consider accepting 100 percent responsibility for the results in his life. If we are going to choose control over our results, we must accept responsibility for them, not just when it serves us, but totally. **If we are not responsible for the results in our lives, who is?**

> Oh! I can tell you who is responsible for the results in my life. It was my father; he was an alcoholic. My mother was too lenient. My brother used to lock me in the closet. My teacher made me write 500 times, "I am a bad boy." My spouse ignores me. My boss never compliments me. My company keeps reorganizing; how do you expect me to feel? It's no wonder I'm not maximizing my potential.

With that mind-set, the only way results will change is if the past changes, the boss changes and the organization changes — fat chance! That is too much control for a person to give away to the past, the boss, or the organization.

●●●

Here is something else to think about. **The results in our lives are with us because there is more benefit to us for having our results as they are than there is benefit to us to change them**. We say we want certain elements of our lives to be different than they are. Yet they remain the same and it frustrates us. Relax, stop being frustrated and stressed out, and acknowledge that because of the way we choose to view positive and negative outcomes, the status quo is chosen. If a person chooses to change, she must accept responsibility for business and personal results in the first place and then choose to do something differently than she is now doing in order to generate different results.

STEPS TO ALTER RESULTS:

1) Be clear as to what current results are.

■ Do a reality check. Watch estimates of your current situation sounding like, "Everything in my life is going to hell in a hand basket." Do you mean "everything?" Everything includes a whole range: emotional, mental, spiritual, social and physical. Also, why in the heck is it going in a hand basket?

2) Be clear as to what desired business and personal results will look like.

■ Allow yourself to be as specific as possible about how each result will look, feel, smell, taste and sound. If you say you want to be a more participative team member, how will you know when you are? List your results in a positive way. An artist would not be very successful if he would approach a blank canvas and say, "This painting will not be of two horses in a field." That approach does not create much of a vision of the final result. Also, attempting to change the results of others is usually futile. We all have enough trouble altering our own results.

3) Be sure you really want the desired result.

■ You asked for the result. Why wouldn't you want it? The question is legitimate. Most of the business/personal results currently experienced in our lives, we have the physical and/or mental ability to change. We could change if we <u>wanted</u> to do things differently or to do different things. Why haven't we?

4) Be prepared to commit yourself to the change.

■ Make a basic choice to possess the desired result. "I formally and officially decide to...." Making this positive commitment on an ongoing basis will direct the subconscious mind to perform the activities needed to accomplish the desired result.

5) Do it!

■ As that old wordsmith, Calvin Coolidge, said, **"We may not be able to do everything at once but we can always do one thing at once."** A hard-to-beat experience is actually making something happen, analyzing the positive and the not-so-positive outcomes and making the needed adjustments.

6) Celebrate!!

■ You have taken a big step by choosing responsibility for your results and control over your results. Do not forget to reward yourself because we get more of the behavior we reward. If it feels good, we are inclined to do it again.

●●●

"Making something happen" brings us to what generates our results, what we do, i.e. behaviors. There is an old Chinese proverb that says, **"If we don't change our direction, we're likely to end up where we are headed."**

To change results, change behaviors. Let us take a look at the next element in the Results Model — behaviors.

Results Model:

Events + Beliefs = Feelings

⇩

BEHAVIORS

⇩

Results

3

BEHAVIORS: IF WE KEEP DOING WHAT WE ARE DOING, WE WILL KEEP GETTING WHAT WE GOT

There once was a manager named Bob. Bob was an inflexible kind of guy. If you asked him to describe himself, he would say, "I am a man of principle. I stick to my convictions." (If he were being brutally honest, he would have to say, "I'm an inflexible kind of guy.") If you asked him how he got that way, he would say, "I've always been that way; my folks are people of conviction too. It runs in the family." When Bob was asked what results in his professional life he would like to alter, he said, "I wish I were as comfortable with change as this other manager in my office." More questioning determined that Brent, Bob's coworker, would consistently generate small changes in his work unit. He was a true learner and was always reading, watching and asking questions. Brent was a master at realigning responsibilities in his work unit to provide the cross training necessary to increase employee self-confidence. He set the reward structure to reward the new and the innovative. When Bob was asked what he did to aid in the introduction of change in his work unit, Bob said, "I come to work, sit at my desk and do today just what I did yesterday and what I hope to be doing again tomorrow. I'm a man of principle and conviction, you know."

Bob would like his results to be different, regarding his relationship with change, but he is not behaving in a way to create the changes he says he wants. If Bob keeps doing what he is doing, he will keep getting what he got. If he changes what he does (his behaviors), he will create different results. They may be better or they may be worse, but they will be different.

●●●

Adam Smith, in his book, *Powers of the Mind*, defines a "paradigm" as "a shared set of assumptions." Smith writes, **"The paradigm is the way we perceive the world; water to fish.** The paradigm explains the world to us and helps us to predict its behavior." The results, Bob and all the rest of us are now enjoying, are the results of the paradigms we have previously established.

Bob sees himself in the world as a routine-oriented kind of a guy. A person buying into that paradigm would naturally exhibit the kind of behaviors that Bob exhibits. Yet Bob says he wants the same results as Brent who is operating within a paradigm of adaptability. Bob has chosen the safety and comfort of keeping within his self-imposed personal image while wishing for the consequences of Brent's behaviors which were designed to be more accepting of change. **The only thing more frustrating than making one choice and wishing for the consequence of another would be to make no choices and to wait around to experience the consequences of other people's choices.**

●●●

Consider the importance of behaviors. Companies do not hire individuals for their values, their belief systems or how they feel about things. **All a company does is rent employees' behaviors**. The company pays X amount of dollars per hour, per week or per month for people to behave in a certain way which over time the company has found will produce the optimal results.

The same is true with a personal relationship. What a person does, i.e. behaviors, will make or break that relationship, regardless of what thinking is involved. Behaviors are how people are judged by the outside world.

●●●

The story of Bob brings up a major point concerning changing behaviors. To change behaviors effectively, one needs to know what a behavior is! To use behaviors to alter results, an individual must think in terms of <u>measurable</u> and <u>observable</u> activities rather than merely characteristics. For our purposes in discussing behaviors and characteristics, let us define a behavior as an action, reaction, or a functioning in a particular way that is measurable and observable and a characteristic as a distinguishing trait, feature, or quality. People often try to change their results with words that have no meaning to their subconscious mind (characteristics) and that part of the mind will ultimately govern the change.

For example, if our friend Bob wakes up in the morning and tells himself that he is going to be more adaptable (a characteristic) that day, when he goes to bed at night, how is he going to know if he was or was not adaptable? Bob, like any of the rest of us if we are to have any significant change in our lives, must be specific as to exactly what needs to be done to accomplish that change. If Bob were to have stated his intentions in more behavioral (measurable and observable) terms such as, "Today I am going to form an interdiscipline project team to enhance group and individual knowledge," he would be well on the way to altering results in the change area of his professional life.

Suppose Bob's boss said Bob's performance was satisfactory in all areas but one and that weakness was he was "inflexible" (a characteristic). To add injury to insult, if Bob did not become more flexible (a characteristic) within three months, the company would no longer require Bob's services.

Might Bob have a question for his boss, a question like, "What do you mean by flexibility?" or "How are you going to know flexibility when you see it?" or "What behaviors should I exhibit?"

●●●

Flexible, innovative, risk taker, empowerer and participative are characteristics used to describe and classify the employee's actions. Characteristics are subjective and difficult to implement to the satisfaction of the boss without some specific behaviors stated or demonstrated and agreed upon.

Mistaking characteristics for behaviors is a common error of many managers when coaching and/or writing evaluations on members of their team. How many managers have told employees to become more motivated (a characteristic)? How is the manager going to know when the employee is motivated? How will the employee know when he has met the manager's expectation?

How about telling a worker in an evaluation that she has a bad attitude (known as having "the BA"), or a good attitude for that matter? Both descriptions are characteristics and, as such, are equally useless for evaluation purposes. With the bad attitude, the person does not know what to do to improve; and with the good attitude, she does not know what to do to maintain that attitude.

We sometimes provide children with the same kinds of vague directions: to be more motivated, assertive, tough, outgoing, and neat or to be less loud, messy, sensitive, aggressive or annoying. Unless we are willing to define specific, measurable and observable behaviors instead of characteristics for ourselves and others, we can not expect to notice long-term positive changes in results.

●●●

Considering this discussion on behaviors versus characteristics, take a minute and look back at "The Fifty-Two" in the introduction of this book.

Would you classify those survey answers as behaviors or characteristics? Hard to find any that are measurable and observable, isn't it? To be fair to the responders of that question, the question was general and general answers were all that were expected. Also without a specific case, defining with measurable and observable activities would have been difficult. But in our personal and professional situations, we do have specific cases and we CANNOT settle for general characteristics.

Managers, telling their employees that to succeed in the changing environment they must be learners, empowerers and/or risk takers and then turning them loose with nothing but characteristics to implement, are performing cruel and unusual punishment. To tell ourselves that we must become more organized and then not to qualify that statement with behaviors is a waste of breath that will result in a waste of time. Understanding the difference between a behavior and a characteristic is obviously more than just a "nice to know" item. **People, wishing to alter results in their personal and professional lives, must program into their daily routine different behaviors than they are currently performing**. This programming activity is difficult enough, but if a person is mistakenly attempting to program a new characteristic rather than a new behavior, change becomes almost impossible.

●●●

Altering a behavior is easier than might be thought. We either do not know how to perform the new behavior, in which case changing behavior is a knowledge issue. Or we do know how and we just do not want to, in which case change is a motivation issue.

Does Bob have the knowledge of the behavior necessary to put together a team? A good test to determine, for yourself or for others, whether you are dealing with a knowledge or a motivation issue is to apply the *Now We Know What You Are Test*. Here is an example of how to apply this test. Suggest to Bob that he form a work team made up of individuals from various disciplines within his organization. Bob's expected response might be, "Oh! I've never done anything like that before. I could never change my method of operation just like that. I'm a man of principle and conviction, you know." Then offer Bob $5,000 to organize the team. If he still can not organize a team, Bob has a knowledge problem.

We know how to handle knowledge problems. For example, Elizabeth's sales results, when dealing with her Hispanic customers who do not speak English, are unsatisfactory. After much deliberation and consultation with her manager, they concluded the problem may very well be that Elizabeth does not speak a word of Spanish. So the behavior she will need to demonstrate, if she is to alter her sales results, is to learn Spanish.

We all know how to learn a behavior. If Elizabeth chooses to learn Spanish, she can: go to class, read books, listen and watch audio and video tapes, observe and model experts, etc. Elizabeth may have some study time ahead to learn Spanish. But consider the possibility that most of the behaviors we need to significantly alter the results in our lives, we, like Bob, already possess.

●●●

Learning to do better what we already know how to do is worth discussion. I conducted a one day workshop on how to prepare and present effective meetings. The participants were all Ph.D.'s from the Research and Development division of a major United States firm. The session started with the question, "What behaviors go into conducting an effective meeting?" For the next five minutes descriptions of what makes up effective meetings poured forth faster than could be put on the flip chart: organizing, planning, and distributing an agenda in advance; adhering to start and end times; keeping participants on task; writing minutes and distributing them in a timely fashion; having the right people in attendance, etc. When the input slowed, looking at this very inclusive list, I asked, "Is there anything on this list you did not know when you came in here or that you currently do not know how to do? If they were not sure they could do the required behavior, the participants were asked to perform the *Forty-Five Caliber Test* (a reverse motivation of *Now We Know What You Are Test*).

The *Forty-Five Caliber Test* is done by placing a forty-five caliber pistol next to the meeting leader's head (figuratively). Then tell the leader, "If you do not prepare an agenda, invite the right participants, start and end the meeting on time and keep the people on the task at hand, parts of your temporal lobe will be found in the next state." Do you think the leader could run an effective meeting? Hard to say for sure, but the smart money is on "Yes!"

Applying the same concept in sales workshops, we ask sales people, "If you were following the top salesperson in your industry, what behaviors would you see him/her performing during each step of the sales process? Could you perform each of those steps better than you are now doing?" Guess what?

The sales seminar participants knew the steps of the sales process. Considering the *Forty-Five Caliber Test*, they could perform each step better than they were presently doing. It is not so much the knowledge required as it is the motivation to apply the knowledge. — *They would do it if they felt like it!*

Results in our lives will happen. They will happen based on what we do or do not do. Therefore our understanding of behaviors, the second link in the Results Model, is critical. The ability to speak Spanish was a behavior Elizabeth did not have but could possess. Bob, on the other hand, possessed a behavior, ability to form a team, that he did not have the desire to apply. Both Elizabeth and Bob have a choice to make. Elizabeth can choose whether or not to learn a new behavior and Bob can choose whether or not to apply an existing one.

That leads us to the next element of the Results Model. Our results are the culmination of our collective choices of behaviors. The behaviors exhibited will be those we feel like exhibiting. Let us move on to feelings.

Results Model:

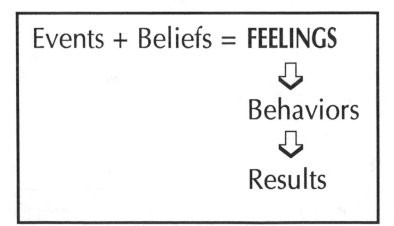

Events + Beliefs = **FEELINGS**
⇩
Behaviors
⇩
Results

4

FEELINGS: A "SOFT" ISSUE IN A "HARD" WORLD

Feelings are the next step in the Results Model. If our results are not the way we want them to be, we should do something differently than we are currently doing. But we will only do something differently if motivated to do it, i.e. if we feel like it.

What is the difference how a person feels as long as he gets the desired results? Some think the subject of feelings is a little "soft" in a business environment. Is not the real issue what gets produced or what the results turn out to be, regardless of our feelings?

Successful results, however defined, are the goal. Only to the extent that feelings contribute positively or negatively to these results, are the feelings important. **When feelings contribute to results, the ability to deal with feelings is, unquestionably, a "hard" skill.**

● ● ●

If feelings are to play any part in an individual's personal and professional life, she must be able to define specific feelings. Creation of the following is a start.

POSITIVE ——————— NEUTRAL ——————— NEGATIVE

The previous continuum of feelings runs from positive through neutral and on to negative. While a person can feel anywhere along this continuum, he will experience only one feeling at a time. A person will not feel positive at the exact same time he is feeling negative, very quickly thereafter possibly, but not at exactly the same time.

Not everyone agrees on precisely where each feeling should be placed on the continuum but below is a list of some common feelings and where the majority of workshop participants place them:

Positive	Neutral	Negative
Good	Indifferent	Angry
Comfortable	Calm	Frustrated
Delighted	Mellow	Mad
Enthusiastic	Serene	Panicky
Vibrant	Cool	Hurt
Happy	Peaceful	Depressed
Excited	Centered	Miserable
Challenged	Temperate	Unfulfilled
Loved	Patient	Uptight
Supported	Tranquil	Confused

Getting back to the original question of how feelings contribute to results — the natural behaviors which follow from anger (generally considered a negative feeling) are different, in the long term, from the natural behaviors that follow from happiness (generally considered a positive feeling).

Notice the words, "natural behaviors." A person can certainly go around behaving as if she is happy, while the truth is that individual is very angry. If the person is into performing unnatural acts, she may be able to carry off "pretending" longer than most folks. Pretending will be discussed further in Chapter Nine. For now, note that **a person who behaves one way and feels another, over the long term, is headed for some heavy-duty stress**.

If a person chooses to spend his present moment feeling frustrated, that negative feeling will drive different behaviors than if the same person had chosen to feel challenged. How do feelings contribute to results? Different behaviors cause different results, and feelings drive behaviors. **If behaviors naturally follow from feelings, why would anyone choose to feel frustrated when he could choose to feel challenged or, at worst, indifferent?**

A person feeling frustration over a proposed change will behave differently over the long run than a person feeling the challenge of change. Different feelings, different behaviors, different results.

> My wife just ran off with my best friend and I sure do miss him. I feel angry and frustrated — how else do you expect me to feel?

What are the mandatory feelings associated with losing a best friend? Negative appears appropriate. Is it not possible that someone may feel neutral or maybe even positive? If a person can envision any of these feelings, then obviously **the feelings are not associated with the circumstance itself but are just some of the many possible feelings available to be chosen**. Do we wish to choose a feeling from the positive, the negative, or the neutral column?

From the Inside Out

Obviously the operative word here is "choose." If a person has not established the paradigm that the choice of how he feels is his, the question is, "*Whose choice is it?*" The answer to that simple question is the difference between someone who is in charge and in control versus someone who spends all waking moments playing the victim and hoping the telephone pole does not come around the corner.

●●●

What people may choose when they find themselves spending too much time in the negative column:

1) Kill themselves — drastic but effective.

We have 35,000 plus suicides a year in the United States and only one out of ten who try suicide succeed! (That may also indicate how strong is the desire for control. An individual can think if life gets too bad, she can always end it.) Drug addicts and alcoholics kill themselves more slowly but just as surely. The desire to avoid spending a prolonged time in the negative feeling column is very strong.

2) Do nothing and accept things the way they are. Put on the hair shirt; start reading the "whine list"; then begin "awfulizing" and "catastrophizing."

3) Pay the price; take control and begin making the tough choices.

●●●

While deciding what to do if you are choosing to spend too much time in the negative column (Hint: Do not choose solution number one. That is a permanent answer to a temporary problem.), here are some thoughts regarding feelings:

■ We pay a price in business when the work environment is not open to discussing feelings. **To cap employees' emotions is to dam up the passion and energy they have to give to the job.** It is unfortunate that the only time some people, who feel their emotions are being stifled, will display any of the passion they have bottled up is when liquor and drugs give them permission. (Could this be why drug and alcohol addiction programs are getting so much attention in business today?)

■ We, as human beings, "felt" on an emotional level long before we "thought" on a cognitive level. When feelings come into conflict with a logical, rational thought, feelings may well elicit a more genuine response. Consider a person's buying motives. The tendency is to buy emotionally and justify the heck out of the purchase rationally, i.e. "I have a family of five and I bought a fire-engine-red, two-seat sports car. This acquisition is a good business decision because the car will have a significant resale value and the purchase is an excellent investment." (Sure, so is a Certificate of Deposit, but it does not come as a red, two-seater!)

When selling the concept of change to others, we must keep in mind how people buy. **We must deal with emotional issues as well as rational issues.**

■ How we feel is at least as important, if not more important, than what we know. *Knowledge is power* may be a maxim embroidered on every doily in the house, but the statement is only half true — *applied knowledge is power.* We may have the knowledge concerning how to function in a changing environment, but how easy is it to apply that knowledge to the fullest long term when we feel angry, frustrated or depressed? **It is difficult to use what "we know" when what "we feel" is unproductive**.

Chapter Three discussed the connection between behaviors and results. If we continue our same behaviors, we will reap the same results. If we wish to change our results, then we change our behaviors. What is being added now is that ultimately, **behaviors will be consistent with feelings**. If we feel enthusiastic, our results will be different, over time, than if we feel depressed because of the behaviors those different feelings generate.

How would it be to deal with people whose behaviors were consistently in alignment with their feelings? We would always know where they stood. If they were angry with us, they would express anger. If they were happy, that also would be expressed. There is a certain beauty in that approach to the world.

How would it feel to be an individual who has confidence enough in his feelings to display behaviors consistently in harmony with those feelings? That is true integrity.

Consider the other possibility — dealing with people whose behaviors over the long run are not consistent with their feelings. With these folks, we are never sure where they stand. This lack of internal integrity is aggravating and irritating for colleagues, but imagine how these confused people must feel! How do you think it would be, over the years, to think you must exhibit behaviors that are out of harmony with what you feel?

Take the case of Gene, a customer service representative in a major corporation. Gene has been serving the customer in the same "follow the rules" style which has served him well for over fifteen years. Recently the president of Gene's company attended a management training workshop providing the list of "Fifty-Two." That experience sold the president on the need for innovative employees for the company to remain effective in the years to come. As we all know, presidents do not stay sold alone. The word quickly spread throughout the organization, "Innovate, or else." Of course, the president never made that statement, but it was perceived and what is perceived, is. Gene, not being the self-destructive kind, began innovating his brains out while feeling unsure of, unhappy with and uncommitted to the concept. Within Gene, disharmony and a lack of integrity existed, creating stress.

My observation is that a lack of harmony between feelings and behaviors is one of the major causes of stress in North American organizations.

If Gene chooses to live in a stressed condition habitually, he can continue to "pretend." He can continue to exhibit behaviors inconsistent with his feelings. He will obtain results consistent with his exhibited behaviors, but at what price?

Consistency between feelings and behaviors benefits our personal well-being. Disharmony over long periods wears a person down.

●●●

Since feelings play such a vital role in obtaining successful results, recognizing feelings, changing them when appropriate, and displaying them in harmony with our behaviors would make sense. To change an unproductive feeling, a person must know where feelings originate. That brings us to the next steps in the Results Model.

Results Model:

EVENTS + BELIEFS = Feelings
⇩
Behaviors
⇩
Results

5

E + B = F: HOW TO CONTROL THE
UNCONTROLLABLE

Where do feelings come from? The formula, E + B = F, may make it easier to put the previous discussion into perspective. Thinking of this formula, reminds me of the story of the ninety-year-old man who went to the priest and told him, "Father, last night I met a twenty-year-old young lady at a bar. I took her to a motel and we made love ten times." The priest said, "For your penance, say ten *Our Fathers* and ten *Hail Marys*." The old man replied, "But Father, I'm not Catholic." The priest asked, "Well, why are you telling me then?" The old man said, "I'm telling everybody!"

Agreed that E + B = F may not appear as exciting to you as the old man's story did to him, but it is more practical.

The F in the formula is feelings. The E stands for the events that occur in one's life. Events are what happen to us during life. **What control do we have over the events in our lives?** By control is meant — the ability to make things happen when we want them to happen, or not make them happen when we do not want them to happen. Looked at in light of that definition, the absolute control one has is very small, if any. For example, before driving to a meeting one block away, a person could get a complete tune up, put on new tires, fill up the gas tank and still not be able to guarantee that the car would make the trip.

We can influence the outcome but we have limited, if any, control.

●●●

The reason many people spend so much time in the negative feeling column is because they make what could be considered a terminal emotional error. They believe that E = F. The belief that events equal feelings leads them to the conclusion that the events in their lives, over which they have little or no control, generate their feelings which drive their behaviors, thereby creating their results. Stated another way, some people do not believe their results to be their responsibility because these results originated from events over which they had no control. These people are assuming a 100 percent victim posture.

Is there a benefit to being a victim? There sure must be. So many people do it. That benefit is — the person now has no responsibility. But the down side is they have given up control. They are giving control over the results in their lives to someone or something over which they have no control — the telephone poles of life.

The issue of what is controllable and what is not controllable is a vital issue. **We do not control the events in our lives. What we do control is what we choose to believe about those events**. And now we have the B in the formula, E + B = F. B equals belief (our own personal paradigm).

●●●

Events in our lives do not cause feelings. What we believe about the events in our lives causes feelings. **This book does not contain a more important concept —— <u>NOTHING HAS ANY MEANING TO US OTHER THAN WHAT WE CHOOSE TO GIVE IT</u>**. We give everything any meaning it has for us.

Is the meaning we are choosing to give to events in our lives empowering us or limiting us?

Taking responsibility for the results in our lives is important, because at some level we have indeed chosen them. For example, a life event occurs. The event is processed through our personal belief system which generates feelings appropriate to the beliefs. Certain behaviors occur which culminate in results. If that same event were to be processed through a different set of beliefs, another paradigm, a different scenario would be put into place. **It is not what happens to us; it is what we choose to believe about what happens to us**. If Lee Iacocca had chosen to believe his firing from Ford meant he was "not a capable person," he might not have moved on to become Le Baron of Chrysler.

The following is an example of how beliefs can affect results:

■ There are three sales people in a sales division. All have been informed the branches are being consolidated with another division. Salesperson Number One has been through a consolidation. As a result she was assigned some lucrative accounts. She chooses to believe the move to be a valuable opportunity. She may even pick up some champagne on her way home. Salesperson Number Two has also been through a consolidation at his last place of employment, which is why it was his last place of employment. He is choosing a much more pessimistic belief than Salesperson Number One. He is choosing to be scared to death and he, like the last little piggy, cried all the way home. Salesperson Number Three is new in the sales position and has never been through a consolidation before; so she is adopting a "wait and see" attitude and will go right home without stopping.

The consolidation of the division is the consolidation of the division. That is all — the consolidation is an event. What the three salespeople choose to believe about that event will initiate their feelings, behaviors, and ultimately their results. **What is important to "get" from this example is the different feelings, behaviors and results were all generated by the <u>same event</u>**. It is not what happens; it is what we believe about what happens.

We now have completed the Results Model — How we get what we got. Let us take a more detailed look at the model.

Results Model:

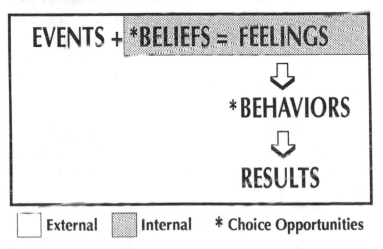

The Results Model is made up of two components, the internal and the external. An external event occurs. The event is processed through the internal belief system which will generate the internal feeling appropriate to that belief which will manifest itself as an external behavior creating an external result. The quality of our results will depend on how well each component of the Results Model is addressed.

The Results Model presents two opportunities for us to make choices — to be in control of our results.

■ The first choice opportunity is internal after an event

occurs. <u>An event occurs</u>. We <u>choose the belief</u> to place on that event. Remember, events do not carry with them mandatory beliefs! That choice of beliefs then creates the appropriate feeling which is always consistent with the belief. That feeling generates a behavior.

■ Here is our second chance to make a choice. We <u>choose the external behavior</u>. We do not have to choose a behavior that is consistent with our feelings. We could pretend. (Caution: This "pretending" can be detrimental to our health and will be discussed in more depth in Chapter Nine.)

Again, **the results in our lives are with us because of the choices we make, first the choice of beliefs (internal) and second the choice of behaviors (external).** The results are not with us because of the events that are a part of everyday life. We choose what we believe about the events that occur around us and we choose what we are going to do about them. We are in control, the random events are not.

●●●

Understanding the Results Model can provide some significant insight into how results are achieved through the alignment of the internal (belief) and the external (behaviors) and the choices made concerning each. Two major areas of action when working with the Results Model:

1) Address both the internal and external.

■ The ability to alter our results, over the long term, depends on our ability and our organization's ability to align and act on both the internal and the external aspects of the Results Model. Traditional training programs deal almost exclusively with the external, i.e. the behaviors. Students are told how to perform tasks designed to accomplish certain results. If they have not committed internally to that skill, they wind up "farming half as well as they know how." Internal commitment is essential for long-term skill implementation. In a previous discussion concerning the workshops conducted on running effective meetings, the participants already knew the skills (external) to run successful meetings. But they had not considered the way their beliefs (internal) may have been limiting the use of those skills.

When attending time-management programs, how many new skills are learned? How many of us know many specific skills we can more fully use to reduce stress, skills to provide more constructive feedback or skills to provide greater support to our team mates? **Skill training is external mastery. Belief training is internal mastery and both are essential for long-term skill implementation.**

2) Deal in behaviors not characteristics.

■ Managers, want very much for their people to succeed, because in reality, the managers get paid for what their people do, not for what the managers do. **The best chance of employees being successful happens when managers define (depending on the worker's degree of maturity) behaviors needed in both measurable and observable terms.**

For example, Helen is a repair technician in a company

undergoing dramatic change. Helen is not taking the change too well. Quite frankly she is lost. She does not understand most of the change. She does not agree with what she does understand and to add to her frustration, she has little or no idea what her job is any more. Helen's manager, trying to help, tells Helen what needs to be done to succeed in their particular changing environment. The manager says Helen needs to improve her communications skills, to learn to manage the process rather than the result and to become more empowered. If this is all the management intervention Helen receives, what is the chance of her success? Her chances are slim to none, considering the external component of the Results Model has been poorly defined. The manager provided characteristics rather than behaviors. The internal component, Helen's belief about change, has not been dealt with at all!

Given the above scenario, watch the Results Model go into action.

Change (event) occurs. Helen believes the change is no good for her personally (belief), so she is frightened one moment and angry the next (feelings). She has been around long enough to know the display of those feelings is not appreciated in her organization. Helen then "pretends" everything is fine. She begins to practice being empowered and managing the process with effective communications skills (behavior) as defined by her.

Consider the possible results. Helen might perform the required behaviors exactly as her manager wants. (Even a blind pig roots up an acorn every once in awhile!) In this case, her results will be satisfactory, but since she is not behaving in harmony with her beliefs, her stress level will rise. This increase in stress level will have a negative effect on her results in the long term.

On the other hand, Helen might not perform the required behaviors exactly as her manager wants. In this case, the boss will let her know. That discussion will raise Helen's stress level even higher than its current high level (because she is still not behaving in harmony with her beliefs) thus causing negative effects on her results in both the long and short run.

●●●

In summary, the Results Model is a potent form for creating either negative or positive results. Its strength lies in our ability to address the internal through recognizing our current beliefs and rethinking them, if appropriate, and in our ability to address the external by defining behaviors rather than characteristics. **If workers do a less than adequate job of dealing with either the internal or the external, long-term results will suffer.**

7

BELIEFS: WHY THEY ARE CRUCIAL IN BUSINESS AND WHERE THEY COME FROM

What we choose to believe is our first response to the events occurring around us and this choice opportunity sets the stage for the implementation of the Results Model. Considering the importance of this first choice, we will now take some time to examine beliefs as they apply to both professional life and personal life.

We, as entities, are made up of two dimensions — body and thought. Thought is how we internally manifest our beliefs. The body is a method of communications. Our bodies convey, or put into effect, our thoughts.

Observing body and thoughts in relation to time, we have a past, a present and a future. Do we exist in the past as both body and thought? No, our past is only alive to us in the realm of thought. When we think about the past, how "real" is that thought?

Ever had a discussion with parents, brothers or sisters about an event that happened when living at home that was very significant to you, and your family either did not remember it happening at all, or saw it in an entirely different light? The question arises, "What really did happen?" **The past is all thought. Is what we choose to believe about the past limiting or empowering actions in the present?**

What about the future, do we exist in thought, body or both? The future, just like the past, exists only in thought. What are our thoughts about our future within the organization, the future of the organization itself, or the future of personal relationships? **Since the future exists only in thoughts, consider if our thoughts about the future are limiting or empowering current actions.** Our choice!

It is this choice of beliefs that gave birth to the concept of "self-fulfilling prophecy." When people are worried about some aspect of the future, those worries are not allowing them to function effectively in the present which is the only time they can do anything at all about the future problem. Such worriers will not have performed the behaviors necessary to bring about a successful result.

For example, Salesperson Number Two in the sales division that was consolidating with another division (discussed in Chapter Five) held a very negative belief concerning the change. He was afraid and angry, afraid about the future, about what might happen, and angry about the past, about what had happened. His feelings, which were created from his beliefs concerning the future and the past, neither of which he can do anything about, are immobilizing him in the present. And the present is the only time he has to put into place the structure needed to give the change any chance of succeeding. When the new environment does not meet his expectations, this sales person will be the first to say, "I told you so."

How about the present, do we exist in body, thoughts or both? Now our act is together. Research has shown that people are most productive when their bodies and minds are in the same place, at the same time. This fact is encouraging but consider just how long that "same time" really is. We only have our bodies and minds in the same place at the same time in the present moment, but this present moment is a different present moment than the present moment was when we started this confusing sentence.

According to the late Buckminster Fuller, who was a futurist, philosopher, engineer, architect and mathematician, human beings are ninety-nine percent nonform. That is ninety-nine percent thought. Even if the percentage were subjective, considering how much of our existence is spent in thought (all of our past, all of our future and all but the fleeting present moments), ninety-nine percent appears realistic.

What if the ninety-nine percent that is nonform is limiting us? We are the only ones who can choose the thoughts that will help maximize our future potential and current productivity. Being less than the best we can be is a tragedy when we are the only "we" there will ever be!

●●●

Another importance of beliefs is how a belief can affect our physiology. For example, consider a subject under hypnosis. When an ice cube is placed on the skin and the subject is told it is a flame, a heat blister will form. Pure thought creating form! Remember in school, there was always at least one sadist in the class, with apparently no nerves and long fingernails, who loved to go to the blackboard, form his hands into bird claws, (It was always a *he*.) start at the top of the board, and slowly and agonizingly run his fingers down the board. His nails would screech down the board not just once, but as many times as he felt was necessary to drive everybody nuts, or until the teacher returned, which ever came first.

What did the thought of that experience of the past do to your body of the present? Any goose bumps or shudders? Any bodily reaction experienced as a result of this description was triggered by pure thought. In the context of those two examples, we can safely say thought creates form. A person choosing negative thoughts, creates negative form in the shape of problems like high blood pressure, ulcers and wet armpits.

●●●

Consider the power of what an individual chooses to believe, both in the total volume of our existence, ninety-nine percent, and in its effect on the body through thought creating form.

The power of what an individual chooses to believe and that choice's effect on results is not a new theory to which the following quotes will attest:

Buddha (563-483 B.C.): **"All we are is a result of what we have thought."**

Epictetus (1st century A.D.): **"We are not troubled by things, but by the opinions we have of things."**

Marcus Arelius (121-180):   **"A man's life is what his thoughts make of it."**

Shakespeare (1564-1616): **"Nothing is good or bad except what thinking makes it so."**

William James (1842-1910): **"The greatest discovery of my generation is that people can alter their lives by altering their attitude of mind. We are not victims of the world we see: we are victims of the way we see the world."**

Mahatma Gandhi (1869-1948): **"A man often becomes what he believes himself to be."**

Facts about personal beliefs:

- They are ours but we did not come into the world with them. Therefore we must have chosen them.

- If we have chosen them, we can "unchoose" them. We do not have to keep them.

- Since we can choose to keep them or not to keep them, we must have control. We are in charge.

A way to summarize the importance of what we choose to believe is that **human beings will behave in accordance with what they believe to be true about themselves and their environment.**

Very basic but essential because our results depend on that choice!

●●●

Considering how important beliefs are to results, we came into this world significantly under-equipped. We did not arrive with a set of beliefs as standard equipment. If we were not born with them, and we have them now, where did they come from? Beliefs are part of an "option package." We get to choose the beliefs with which we operate.

The late B.F. Skinner said, "**Society attacks early, while the individual is helpless**." From the time we come home from the hospital, society, in its many forms, supplies input to our belief systems.

The initial input, of course, is from parents, followed by input from everybody and everything else: friends, teachers, coworkers, religion. The list is almost endless. All of our lives' experiences affect our belief systems in varying degrees. A very powerful input in establishing short-term beliefs is the media. The media tell us how to smell, how to dress, where to go on vacation, the "in" way to talk, where to live and even what tastes good.

Consider all of the inputs to our belief systems on a daily basis and realize that all of these outside experiences are bombarding us with potential beliefs. We choose which beliefs to let in, but we do not have to keep them, therefore, we have control. Beliefs we choose to bring in, we give a home in our belief systems. From that day forward, until we choose to change, our lives will be conducted as if "that is the way things are." **Are the beliefs we are**

choosing to adopt, empowering or limiting us? Our choices!

●●●

Note: The remainder of this chapter was written for managers or for those who aspire to be managers, but the points are valid for all readers.

The way an individual chooses to view the world is personal choice. The way a manager chooses to view the job as manager is also personal choice. Assuming people were not born with beliefs concerning how to manage, where did those management paradigms originate?

If you are a manager now, do you remember when you were promoted into management? Here is how it happened to me. My boss called me into his office and said I was being promoted to management, "Congratulations and good luck!" After the obligatory grovelling, I left the office to begin being a leader of human beings.

Does that approach sound familiar? What if my manager had told me, instead of being promoted, I had been chosen to drive the pole position at that year's Indy 500 race. Might I have had an additional question for him like, "Just how do I do that?" The question, "How do I do managing?" never came up when I was promoted, and I don't believe my situation was all that unusual.

Where do managers learn to be managers? Where do they get their beliefs concerning the purpose of the management job: by instinct, workshops, seminars, formal schooling, audio/video tapes, books, observation of other managers?

Does a manager know how to manage by instinct? A born manager is somewhat like a born brain surgeon. There are innate abilities both possess making them good at their professions, but most people would not like either the surgeon or the manager plying her trade on them without a little more going than "gut feeling."

Are workshops, seminars and formal classes where a manager learns how to manage? My belief is that people become "aware" of how to manage in classrooms. They are exposed to effective management behaviors, but do not actually "learn."

Are audio/video tapes and books the answer? The advantages and limitations of these materials are the same basically as for classroom activities. All of these approaches to learning the management role are awareness events. These events are designed to place the responsibility on the learner to develop on the job in areas he feels improvement is necessary.

What part does observing other managers play in the development of management technique? If you are one of the lucky ones to have had your manager spell out exactly how she saw your role and you are still working for that person, for appraisal purposes, you may wish to consider incorporating that information into your management role definition. If your role has not been spelled out to your satisfaction, other state-of-the-art means, such as talking to your manager, will have to be employed. Without a clearly defined role, managers have to decide for themselves, every day, what behaviors to exhibit.

Without being born managers, manager behavior has to be acquired from someplace. Managers have received, to some degree or another, input from many of the sources mentioned. They have been exposed to workshops, seminars, formal classes, books, tapes, written job definitions and role models. Those experiences created what managers believe they should be. This choice of belief about the management role is a very basic but important decision, because human beings always behave in accordance with what they believe about themselves and their environment.

●●●

Following is an example of how managers may behave:

Bill's first job as a manager was as a management trainee, the first person hired directly into management to ride the fast track at the Pittsville Sausage Company's bratwurst division.

When accepting his initial assignment, Bill found the youngest person reporting to him had twenty years of sausage service. The oldest was young when the Dead Sea was just sick. Bill had what might be referred to as a mature work force.

The majority of Bill's time in college was not spent learning bratwurst or management. The position in which he believed himself to be, was that his people had all the knowledge while he had all the authority. Bill quickly recognized that to get work done with and through his team, he needed to develop a participative management style to survive while developing his people. Bill believed that about himself and his environment. Therefore he behaved as if this were true.

Fred is another example of entering into the management ranks. Fred was the most technically competent worker in his group. When it came time for Fred's boss to move on to bigger and better things, the knighthood of management was bestowed upon Fred who was, after all, the most technically competent. Fred, and every one in his group, knows why he was promoted. What aspect of the job does Fred believe defines his management role? Fred believes he is Supertech! He will now behave as if that were true.

Following Bill and Fred further, watch what happens. In today's work environment, especially in the technical side, change occurs rapidly. How long would Fred have to be out of his former role before the technical aspects of the job would start to change? Fred soon may be unable to answer a technical question from one of his people.

What does that cause in Fred? He is drop kicking pigeons on the way home from work, not because of what is actually happening, (an employee asking for help) but because of what Fred believes about what is actually happening. Fred believes he is a failure as a manager because he can not do what he perceives he was promoted to do, be a technical expert. A technical question could have been asked of Bill who does not believe himself to be Supertech and he would go home his same sweet, old, lovable self. A person will "feel" in accordance with what he believes. How might Fred and Bill behave in accordance with their respective paradigms?

If an employee came up to Bill, a "developing people" type of manager, and asked for help filling out a new form, what behaviors might Bill perform? Consistent with his belief of the role of a manager as a people developer, he could review the form with the employee and give possible suggestions as to where the employee might find out for himself how to correctly fill out the form. When the form is filled out correctly, Bill and the employee might have another little informal meeting to ensure mutual understanding so in the future this problem will not arise, or will at least be minimized. This approach may seem time-consuming, and it is — up front, but over the long term, it is a time-saver.

What behaviors might we expect from a manager such as Fred who views his job as Supertech? Consistent with his belief concerning his role in results attainment, Fred may say, "Bring that form here. I'll fill it out for you." This response is consistent with Fred's belief about his Supertech role and reinforces his belief by:

1) Reestablishing his technical superiority.
2) Getting the job done quickly — good short-term results!

Neither a Supertech or a People Developer approach is necessarily right or wrong. They just are. The question is, are they appropriate, considering the makeup of the manager's team and the results to be accomplished? **What the manager believes to be his or her role will drive the**

manager's behaviors. Basic but essential!

• • •

Managers who have ever been surprised by, or who have surprised anyone else with, a performance appraisal can confirm it was not one of the highlights of their careers. One of the reasons this highly undesirable situation occurs is because the manager and the subordinate have not discussed required behaviors at length. For example, a manager may see her role as Supertech and conduct all daily activities consistent with that belief. Her manager sees the role as a developer of people and produces appraisals consistent with that belief. What we have here is a "failure to communicate." We have an appraisal given to a person who could swear it belonged to somebody else!

What happens if there is not communication between a manager and the people reporting to him concerning how the manager views the manager's job? Ann believes herself to be a developer of people. The people Ann sees herself developing, see Ann as Supertech and look for Supertech behaviors from her.

Charlie, one of Ann's team, desired a Supertech manager and came to Ann for help in filling out the form mentioned earlier. She sat Charlie down and showed him how to find out for himself. When he left the office, Charlie did not feel as if his manager did her job.

Reverse the roles. Charlie wants a developer of people as a manager and Ann is sitting around filling out the form for him. An equally undesirable experience!

●●●

"People Developers" and "Supertechs" obviously are not the only two roles managers practice. These roles provided examples of two different beliefs and emphasized the importance of what managers choose to believe about the conduct of management behavior.

The most effective managers have chosen to define their roles as some flexible combination of both, with maybe a few other roles thrown in. If you are a manager,

> How do you define your role?
> What input did you use to define your role?
> Is your defined role working?
> Will your current role definition work in a changing
>   environment?

These are basic questions and the answers are essential.

●●●

The importance of beliefs in business and personal life has been discussed. How thoughts affect physiology has been illustrated. **You choose beliefs and you can change them if they are not helping to achieve the results you desire**.

8

SELF-TALK: A CRITICAL CONFERENCE

Our personal and professional beliefs begin external to us as events. A person would have to take a good look in the mirror to see who gives beliefs their credibility and their permanence.

Everybody on the face of the earth can tell us that we are not intelligent enough to survive in a changing environment. Until we tell ourselves that we are not intelligent enough, we are veritable Einsteins. (Albert Einstein, Incidentally, flunked math in school and chose not to buy into the low intelligence belief.) *You telling yourself* is technically dubbed "sub-vocalization" which most of us know as, talking to ourselves or self-talk.

An example of the importance of what we tell ourselves in words (self-talk) or in pictures (visualization) can be found in the story of Colonel George Hall. Colonel Hall, a prisoner in solitary confinement in Viet Nam for seven years, shot a golf round of seventy-six less than one week after his release. When asked how he could play golf so well after not having played in seven years, Colonel Hall answered, "That's all I did for seven years."

For seven years Colonel Hall, in his mind, replayed every golf course he had ever played and every great shot he ever made. When the Colonel stood over that golf ball for the first time in seven years, his subconscious mind, the control for all automatic body responses, was ready. It had been playing golf every day for seven years — and it was good!

Experimental and clinical psychologists have stated that the human mind does not tell the difference between actual experience and an experience imagined vividly and in detail. Colonel Hall did not actually play golf, but he did imagine it vividly and in detail.

●●●

If we are to maximize our potential, we must program ourselves with empowering thoughts. **What do we say to ourselves about our ability to cope with change?**

Notice what happens when we use negative self-talk. A person thinks at an average rate of approximately 1,000 words per minute. If only ten percent of those words are negative, that is 100 negative words per minute or 6,000 negative words per hour x sixteen waking hours = 96,000 negative words being fed into the subconscious mind which believes everything "imagined vividly and in detail."

●●●

Game time — complete these sentences.

"Pepsi cola hits the_____."
"Ivory soap is_____."
"Call for_____."

Now that many of us have shown our age, when is the

last time we have heard any of those commercials? Maybe twenty or thirty years ago, and even then we didn't listen for them. We were probably going to get a sandwich or to the bathroom. Yet many years later, you are sitting in your nice cozy chair saying, to yourself hopefully, "Spot.... Ninety-nine and 44/100 percent pure.... Philip Morris."

Not only does the subconscious mind believe everything imagined vividly and in detail, it also remembers everything forever!

●●●

Many of us would not talk to others, or let others talk to us, the way we talk to ourselves. When we talk, who is always there to hear us? We are always available for a conference. That is both good news and bad news. There will be more discussion later about how damaging negative self-talk can be. For now it is important to remember that, **while beliefs may originate externally, they are reinforced internally. We choose whether that reinforcement is empowering or limiting current actions.**

●●●

Your mission, if you choose to accept it, is to help an alien from another planet to be assimilated in your world, but the alien is having a problem. The planet the alien comes from, Utopias, is populated by only happy, joyful, fulfilled beings and because of this constant cheerful, optimistic outlook, the alien is easily recognizable by most earthlings. To avoid the detection of your new friend, you will need to help it be more like us.

With that direction, participants in our workshops are asked to help the alien be more like us by being more stressed by change. First, the group participants tell the alien what it should be thinking and saying to program itself to "stress out" at the first sign of change. Sample negative self-talk:

- "I don't have the skill to succeed in the new environment."
- "I have too many other things to do to bother learning something new."
- "It's just the beginning of the end.
- "I liked the old way better."
- "I'll never be able to adjust."
- "Nobody asked me and this new way doesn't make sense."
- "We're going through all this and it's not going to work anyway."
- "I've been around too long to try something new."
- "If upper management ever figured out what they were doing they would be dangerous."
- "We tried this before and it didn't work. Why do they think it will work now?"

Next, we ask the participants to explain and demonstrate how the alien should appear to others, i.e. what behaviors it should exhibit when stressed by change. (No sense being all bent out of shape over change if you can't show it.)

- Walk around shaking your head.
- Let out a big, deep sigh about every ten seconds.

- Scrunch up your face.
- Throw a temper tantrum over small inconveniences.
- Keep all new information to yourself. There is no telling when you might need it.
- Smile out of context.
- Fight even the smallest turf battle to the death.
- Throw darts at the new organization chart.
- Put the pension department on your speed dialer.

While this exercise is fun, it has a serious point. In every situation where the alien exercise has been conducted, the participants do not experience any problems knowing what to say or what to do to intensify the negative feelings toward change.

People were not born with a fear of change. (As a matter of fact, it has been stated that the only person who likes change is a wet baby.) If we have negative feelings concerning change as adults and did not have negative feelings as children, we are therefore choosing to let negative feelings in by internalizing the negative self-talk. (Not a good idea considering the subconscious mind believes everything imagined vividly and in detail.)

We have met the enemy and it is us! People teach themselves to be negative as surely as they could have taught the alien — by using the negative self-talk and exhibiting the negative behaviors.

●●●

We know just what to say and what to do to put ourselves under negative stress. That is the bad news, but if we have taught ourselves how to be negative using limiting self-talk, we can teach ourselves to be positive using empowering self-talk. That is the good news. We are back in control.

STEPS TO REPHRASE SELF-TALK IN ORDER TO ALTER RESULTS:

Our beliefs originated externally and were given their energy and emotion by being accepted internally through self-talk. If the self-talk and visualization we are engaging in is not, as a natural outcome, producing the results desired, it is time to re-phrase.

1) State specifically what you want.

■ "I am a success in this company." That statement is much too broad and will leave you wondering if you have what you want, and if not, when did you lose it. "I am the General Manager at forty-five years of age." Stated in this way, the subconscious mind has a focus upon which to concentrate.

2) State new self-talk in the first person.

■ You are the one whose results you are attempting to alter. While the desire to change other people is strong, it is not the best use of your time. Self-talk such as, "My boss recognizes my contribution to the team's success," might be a worthwhile result, but that recognition is up to your boss, not you.

3) State new self-talk in the positive.

74

■ Tell yourself what you want, not what you do not want. It is difficult to focus on a negative. "I don't want to get all stressed out." That statement is understandable, but it is what you do not want to be. What do you want to be? Consider stating, "I am a calm, relaxed person."

4) State what you want as if it has already happened.

■ "I am the General Manager." (Caution: Step 4 is strictly self-talk and not to be stated out loud or they will be locking you up before you do become the General Manager.) This step is controversial. There are those who say we should not lie to ourselves. But don't we sometimes lie to ourselves when we program in negative self-talk? "I'm too stupid to walk and chew gum at the same time!" The subconscious mind, which will direct automatic body functions toward our stated end, would not be sure when to start us doing "General Manager things" if we program it with, "I will be a General Manager when I'm forty-five years old." Stating what is desired as if it has already happened allows us to internalize a visual picture of having already accomplishing our goal.

5) State your new self-talk in writing.

■ Repeating our desired result exactly the same each time keeps us on track. The new self-talk should be read daily just after getting up in the morning and just before going to sleep at night.

9

STRESS: A NATURAL OUTCOME OF PRETENDING

The first choice opportunity in the Results Model is what a person chooses to believe about events. What she chooses to do about those events (behavior) is the second choice opportunity. The concept of the Results Model is based on the assumption that people's behaviors will be consistent with what they believe, but are there not people who believe one way and act another? Don't we all do it every once in awhile?

We all act with a lack of harmony between our beliefs and our behaviors periodically over the short term. **What would happen to us if consistently, and over the long term, we chose to behave differently than we believe we should behave?** As was mentioned earlier, it is my belief that this lack of harmony is a major cause of negative stress. People who, day in and day out, behave on their jobs or in a particular relationship, in opposition with what they believe, know the destructive nature of that inconsistency. (Note: There is positive stress. We need stress just to get up in the morning. The technical, medical term for a total lack of stress is — dead.)

Remember Fred, the Supertech manager, from Chapter Seven? He truly believes his job is to help his people become technically proficient through example. After all that is why Fred was promoted, wasn't it? Fred's upper management recognizes a need to alter organizational management style if the business is to remain competitive in a changing business environment. Training sessions, meetings, memos, a new team concept and a change in reward structures are designed by the executives to move the overall company management style from directive to coaching. Fred is a survivor. He has been with the company too long not to recognize a need to change his behaviors, but he is not worried. He has been through this "management by best seller" before. Fred has "seen them come and seen them go." He will just wait this out.

In the meantime he will spend each day behaving like a coach by mutually getting agreement on the problem with his workers, mutually discussing solutions, mutually agreeing on actions, following up and rewarding, but in his mind he is still — Supertech! It is hard to say how long Fred can last with this lack of integrity between what he believes and what he does. Sooner or later, the negative stress will drive him to either change his mind concerning the benefits of being a coach or he will revert to his directive ways, but a change will happen. The negative stress is too excessive to pretend over the long term.

●●●

"So what's a little negative stress? That's what we get paid the big bucks for, isn't it?" Let us examine the negative stress caused by pretending.

> Once upon a time there was a cave man named Grog who woke up especially hungry one morning. He rolled away the rock in front of his cave and headed out to hunt a dinosaur for breakfast. (This

fellow deserves credit for ambition and a healthy dose of self-confidence for hunting dinosaurs because the decoy alone weighed over three tons.)

Grog was about ten steps in front of the mouth of the cave when he came eyeball to eyeball with the only thing hungrier than he out that morning — the meanest looking saber toothed tiger a cave man would ever care to meet. Recognizing a win/lose situation when he saw it, Grog decided that he was not that hungry after all. Maybe he would just go back in the cave, tidy up and make his bed, trim his beard, comb the hair on his back, kind of make it an "in the cave day," just mellow out. This was not his day. As Grog turned to head back into the cave, between the cave opening and him, stood the largest woolly mammoth elephant in recorded history. Granted, there was not a lot of history at that time, but it was still one big elephant.

There stood Grog. Right in front of him was a saber-toothed tiger, who Grog was sure wanted to eat somebody. Grog was not sure the tiger wanted to eat him, but he was also not willing to take the chance on mistaken identity. In back of Grog was the elephant the size of a domed stadium.

What goes on in the body of our cave man friend under these circumstances, besides the complete evacuation of his bowels and bladder?

- Hypothalamus activates the pituitary gland. The pituitary gland releases a chemical called ACTH. An immediate chain reaction is set off within the endocrine system.

- Adrenalin is produced by using sugar and stored fats.

- Coagulation chemistry kicks up.

- Digestive system shuts down.

- Pupils dilate and eyelids open wide to optimize vision.

- Skin surface blood vessels contract causing the skin to pale.

- Perspiration increases; goose bumps occur and hair stands on end to maximize body cooling.

- Muscles contract to prepare for immediate movement.

- Liver releases glucose into the blood stream to fill the muscles.

- Spleen pumps blood cells into the accelerated blood circulation so the respiratory system can gulp more oxygen.

- Senses are sharpened.

- Blood pressure rises.

- Sperm production shuts down (because Grog should not need that function at this time).

In all, over 1,400 known physiochemical reactions occur under periods of severe stress.

What happens in the body of a modern human?

Susan walks into her office, and the telephone receptionist greets her by saying that waiting on the phone, for Susan only, is her company's biggest customer. The client is not happy. As a matter of fact the receptionist feels the only way the client would be appeased is if he received Susan's right hand via overnight mail. On the long walk to the telephone, a walk that is reminiscent of the death march at Bataan, Susan's boss's secretary stops her. The secretary says the boss would like Susan to clean out her desk and when she gets home, she should give the boss a call. He said it was important.

What do you think goes on in the body of a modern day human in these circumstances? The hypothalamus activates the pituitary — right down the line. We are living in the space age with stone age biochemistry, and while most of us are not generally in constant physical danger, some people choose "to see the tiger" every day.

Hans Selye, the famous stress researcher, told us what happens with constant "tiger sightings." He called it the General Adaptation Syndrome — which has the acronym of GAS. (Hans Selye had a sense of humor!) The General Adaptation Syndrome defines four stages of stress:

1) Alarm — The fight or flight response we just described.

2) Resistance — The body is not designed to have 1,400 unnecessary chemical changes occurring often. The body begins to resist.

3) Exhaustion — As the body resists the alarm stage over time, physiological systems begin to break down.

Doctors see this stage as:
> Hypertension
> Heart Attacks
> Colitis
> Ulcers

Therapists see this stage as:
> Anger
> Rage
> Frustration
> Depression

4) Termination — The death of the organism. People die as a result of prolonged stress.

To reduce negative stress thereby increasing personal and organizational productivity, we must stop:

■ Choosing to "see the tiger" if there is no tiger.

■ Acting with a lack of harmony between our beliefs and our behaviors.

We must stop, in a word, pretending.

10

REFRAMING: HISTORY NEED NOT BE DESTINY

How do we stop pretending? How is consistency regained between what is believed and what is done? We either raise the bridge or lower the river, i.e. change our beliefs or change our behaviors. Supertech Fred can be an example.

Fred can either change his paradigm concerning the purpose of his job from that of a technician to a coach, to be more consistent with the required coaching behaviors, or he can change his behaviors back to be consistent with his Supertech belief. The choice is Fred's!

Since ultimately beliefs and behaviors must be consistent for good mental health, let us concentrate on changing beliefs to become consistent with the required behaviors needed to accomplish desired results.

If for no other reason, reexamining beliefs is worthwhile because of the passage of time. **Beliefs chosen in the past will be lived in the future. If the future looks like it might be different from the past, maybe different beliefs will be necessary**. While changing a belief (a paradigm shift) may not be the easiest activity, it is sometimes practical, certainly in Fred's case.

●●●

Chapter 10 —— Reframing

View the mind as a wall of Post Office boxes with each box filled with specific information which will remain unless new information comes in to destroy or replace it. How do we choose what information to change and what to leave alone? How do we choose what beliefs to change and what to leave alone?

Many people choose by default. There is so much out there from which to choose we get confused and do what we did the last time. Therefore, **since only the past is known, because the past is all that is available to us, our past beliefs will control our present feelings and behaviors unless we use all our current rational abilities to program ourselves in another direction.** The past brought us to the present, but it does not have to take us to the future. This programming operation involves "letting go," not an easy process.

> The story is told about a man, who while on a hike by himself, fell over a 100 foot cliff. On his way to certain destruction, or at least some major black and blue marks, he was fortunate enough to grab a vine sticking out of the side of the cliff. That was the good news. The bad news was he was still about seventy-five feet from the bottom. He knew neither he nor the vine were planning to spend the night in that position. He had to do something. So he yelled at the top of his lungs, "Is there anyone up there who can help me?" The clouds began to swirl, bubble and then part. A deep voice said, "I am the Lord. I will help you, but first you must trust me and let go of the vine." The man stared at the parted clouds for a minute, then he looked down

seventy-five feet to the jagged rocks below. He looked back up and said, "Is there anybody else up there who can help me?"

Letting go is not an easy process, but it is a requirement if a person is to alter existing results. The choice is ours, our option.

●●●

Strong people rarely run out of options. They almost never lock themselves into one way of believing or behaving. There is more than one way to view any situation. Some ways events are viewed will empower us and help us accomplish our objectives while other views will, at best, limit us and, at the worst, stop us in our tracks.

If we find ourselves in possession of a belief that is not allowing us to maximize our potential because the belief is creating negative stress, we need to get rid of the belief. Definitely easier said than done, but it must be done! Unproductive beliefs must be taken and viewed in a way that will encourage success. **Beliefs must be reframed so they trigger positive feelings which will trigger the behaviors needed to alter results positively.**

Following are some playful examples of reframing beliefs:

■ What is usually said while examining one of those insurance charts that tell how much you should weigh for your height? "I'm not too heavy; I'm just too short."

■ How about, "I don't have a receding hairline; I have a

proceeding forehead."

■ We own some property in northern New Mexico. When people ask me how much, I usually tell them, "It's only an acre and a half, but it's 4,000 miles deep!"

■ One of my favorite reframing stories is about a general who was advised of some bad news by his officers. The general was told that he and his troops were surrounded by the enemy. The general's reaction was, "That's good! Now we can attack in any direction!"

We must see the world in a way which empowers us, not in a way which limits us. Start by doing what the general did. When someone approaches with some "bad news," say, "That's good!" Then try to figure out why. That exercise projects us into the future with a plan rather than immobilizing us in the present which is the only time we have to do anything about the bad news.

PERSONAL REMOTE CONTROL

Recently, I was sitting at home watching television. Actually, I wasn't watching television. I was attempting to set the Guinness world record for *Whipping Through All Available Cable Channels in the Shortest Time Using a Remote Control From the Standard Couch-Potato Position.* Unfortunately, the current record is jointly held by my two sons when they lived at home. It is a good bet that no one will ever come close to beating it in our life time. It was worth a shot anyway.

On PBS there was a documentary on the nostralamus

gland and its part in aiding nose hair growth. More news than I wanted to know was on CNN. ESPN had on a billiards and bowling double-header. My quest for the record was temporarily put on hold when I hit the Weather Channel. The discussion of the five-day forecast for Holland really grabbed my interest.

There is a reason for this story.... As I watch the Weather Channel, is CNN still on? Of course. I have just chosen not to tune it in. **In our lives we each have our own remote control to "tune in" what we want to let in.**

If we believe that people are basically selfish and dishonest, what do you think we will find when we go out into the world? Sure, selfish and dishonest people. Are they out there? Yes, but are there not also giving and honest people? To whom do we choose to tune our remote control? If we believe that by nature, upper management is secretive and not worthy of trust, what will we find in our dealings with company executives?

Have you ever watched young children, even those old enough to know better, giving their Christmas lists to the most ragtag Santa Claus one could imagine, the one with the string from his beard visible over his ears and the moustache down around the lower lip? What does that child see? Just what she believes. The same is true for us "older kids."

Reframing our beliefs is like pushing another button on our remote controls hoping to bring in a better "station," a station that will help us maximize our productivity. For example, if an individual's remote control is set on the belief that says, "Any job worth doing is worth doing perfectly," does that "setting" or belief empower a person? That belief empowers a person by insuring he will do the best at what ever he chooses to do. How does that belief limit a person? Well, Rudy never lost a major tennis tournament. Rudy also never entered a major tennis tournament. If Rudy has the belief that any job worth doing is worth doing perfectly, and if he does not think he can play tennis perfectly, he will not even try. Major limitation!

If our remote controls are set on beliefs that are doing us good, we should stay with them. For example, I believe I should not walk blindfolded down the busiest street in town at rush hour. I also believe that people should never play poker with someone whose first name is the same as a city. These beliefs have served me well!

We tune out everything that is not of value or a threat to us. **When we shift our paradigms, we let in things that were out there all the time,** and like the kids with the poor excuse for a Santa Claus, we just didn't choose to see them.

Every once in a while, change the station on your remote control. What is out there is really interesting!

STEPS TO ALTER RESULTS
THROUGH BELIEF REFRAMING

1) Recognize and label specifically any negative feeling which is leading to less than effective behavior.

■ To label a negative feeling specifically is not always as

simple as it sounds. "Am I angry or is it frustration that I feel?" Being clear on the exact feeling will make it easier to trace the belief that is causing the negative feeling.

2) Identify the event that seems to lead to the feeling.

■ Most often when we find ourselves feeling in the negative column, we can go back to a point in time when we felt either positive or neutral. We can then figure what happened to change that feeling. What was the event? "I was going great guns all day until my boss asked me if I had my résumé updated!"

3) Identify your beliefs concerning that event.

■ Tough job! The beliefs may be deeply buried, but, obviously, to change them we need to know what they are. If you were panicky when asked if your résumé was updated, what is your belief about the meaning behind the question?

4) Ask yourself the following questions:

a. Is this belief consistent with observable fact?

Step outside of yourself or, better yet, ask someone else whose opinion you respect to look at the situation objectively.

b. Could I be mistaken about this belief?

Remain open to the possibility that there might be another way to view this belief.

c. Would everyone else in this same situation feel the same?

Easy answer — no.

d. Is it helpful for me to hang on to this belief?

This question calls for a logical answer, but coming to grips with the answer emotionally may take awhile.

5) Replace limiting beliefs with empowering beliefs.

■ If beliefs you now are choosing to hold are not productive, consider reframing them through the use of STEPS TO REPHRASE SELF-TALK IN ORDER TO ALTER RESULTS found in Chapter Eight.

SECTION TWO

Reducing the Roadblocks to Effective Change

11
ROADBLOCKS OR STEPPING STONES

In Section One, the Results Model was introduced. An event happens. We choose a belief about that event. From that chosen belief comes a feeling. Out of that feeling we choose a behavior, either a behavior that is consistent or inconsistent with the natural feeling. From that chosen behavior, a result is generated. Also discussed was how we came to integrate our beliefs into our lives through external sources (parents, friends, family, experiences, media, etc.) and from a powerful internal source (self-talk).

What is learned can be unlearned. If the paradigms we have made available to ourselves from which to choose are of the type that are limiting our potential, we can alter those limiting beliefs through reframing.

Section Two is designed to provide input for reframing our beliefs (if that is necessary) concerning four major personal and professional life Issues. Those issues are change, failure, security and self. These four were chosen because my experience in working with organizations going through change has convinced me that if we choose negative beliefs concerning these issues, they will present insurmountable roadblocks to the effective management of change.

We are living in a changing world, which by its very

nature can produce failures, temporary business/personal relationships and self-doubt. If we are choosing negative beliefs about these four issues, we are also choosing masochism.

●●●

What people choose to believe about each of these important issues may cover the continuum from being severely depressed to being euphorically giddy. The important fact is: where you choose to be on the continuum does not matter. There is no universal right or wrong belief concerning change, failure, security and self.

    A. Change produces growth and learning.

    B. Change produces uncertainty and confusion.

Which is correct, (A) or (B)? They both are. The point is **if we are living in a world of change and choose to tune in the negative belief on our remote control, we are setting up the Results Model to work against our chances of attaining positive results**. If we choose the positive belief, which is also right, our chances of success are significantly increased. **Is what we are choosing to believe working**?

Since an objective of this book is to release individual potential to increase the power of the organizational structure to accommodate change, this section will deal with the issues of the pain of change itself and its three offspring: fear of failure, fear of potential loss of security and self-doubt.

CHANGE: AND OTHER HAZARDS OF GROWTH

Misoneism — a noun meaning hatred, fear or intolerance of innovation or change.

Isn't that convenient? We have a dictionary definition for the people to use if they have negative beliefs about change.

Why change is greeted by some with neutrality and by others with passionate negativism is easy to understand. Only the past is known. During periods of change we are giving up something known for something unknown. Not always considered a good trade! Only if we are uncomfortable, because of the old, will the risk of going for the new even remotely hold any appeal. Happily skipping into change also appears unlikely considering the good we have now is present and certain, while the promised good is delayed and a gamble — not a very motivating force to make a move.

Why would anyone ever choose change? As stated, only if there is more perceived discomfort attached to the status quo. Everything we do is done because we perceive the activity to be in our own best interests. **Change will not occur unless it is easier for individuals to change than not to change**. So what is the fuss about change? If we do not wish to change, we will not change. Of course, we experience the consequences which in choosing not to change could be our very emotional and/or physical survival and in choosing change could be the immediate dis-comfort of the unfamiliar. But since the choice to change or not is ours, let us get comfortable with the change we choose.

●●●

Marion's boss, after careful market analysis, decided that the company could better serve the existing client base if, rather than assigning sales accounts by geography, the boss would assign the accounts by industry. Marion's work world has now changed. What are her choices?

Since this book is not meant to be a James Michener "mega-novel," let us just stick with some of Marion's obvi-ous choices.

■ She can choose to go along with the new direction in both her beliefs and her behaviors thereby focusing her energy and maximizing her results.

■ Marion can choose to believe organizing by industry is a bad move. Because she has become accustomed to eat-ing and has tied that activity to the successful completion of her job, she will behave as if she believes the change to be a good idea. This choice will increase Marion's negative stress and reduce her productivity.

■ She can choose to believe the change to be the worst idea she has ever heard and tell her bosses what she thinks. Marion's behaviors and beliefs are now in harmony. But is there harmony between Marion and her manage-ment?

All of Marion's potential choices have consequences. She will examine each consequence and choose the approach she perceives is in her best interests. If Marion does not believe in the change, she can choose to either tell her boss or not to tell her boss. Each approach has its pluses and minuses. If she tells, she has integrity but may strain the relationship she has with her boss. If she keeps it to herself, she keeps the relationship intact, but internal harmony is strained.

Marion, and only Marion, will choose in which direction she will go. So, if she chooses not to relay her displeasure, let us hope that Marion will not go around moaning about the change. She chose not to do anything about it! What Marion chose was designed, given all the alternatives she could envision, to be in her best interest.

●●●

Being happy with change may be easier written than done because the move from the familiar to the less familiar is to some degree stressful. Most people today have probably had the opportunity to listen to someone wrestling with the stress of change. It is almost guaranteed that somewhere in the conversation the words, "not in control" or "not in charge" arose. This belief that we are not in control of the change happening in our lives tends to raise negative stress. (Of course, the fact that we <u>are not</u> in control of the change events that occur in our lives does little to reduce that stress!)

The importance of this thought process, as it relates to our attitude concerning change, is that change is viewed as a negative when we do not perceive ourselves in charge of initiating it. However change is considered as an exciting challenge when the change was initiated by us. <u>We are now in control, in charge</u>.

It is not that change happens. It is what we believe about change happening. This fact should make everybody feel better about change. **While the change event may not always be within our control, what we choose to believe about change and what we choose to do about it, definitely is. We are in control. We are in charge**.

●●●

When people choose to set their remote controls to the negative view of change, and the inevitable change happens, it comes across to them as a threat. Their responses will naturally be defensive. When this defensive posture is assumed, their main objective is to resist the change. Maybe the change will go away. The defenses used to resist change are many and varied. Two possibilities are climbing into a box and refusing to discuss any aspect of the change, or ripping the lips off anyone who attempts to discuss change.

A person can also behave like Mr. or Ms. Cooperation and tell everybody that the change looks like a good idea but continue to go about stonewalling the change. Another reaction could be to run away, mentally or physically, from the whole concept. These different responses are all designed to accomplish the main objective of the defensive person — to make change go away.

On the other hand, when people set their remote controls to view change in a more neutral to positive light, change comes across as a challenge or an opportunity. The response will be more accepting. When someone is willing to accept even the remotest possibility that the "agent of change" may have some validity, he begins to become actively involved in the process of change. That involvement does not come alone. With the involvement, at any level, comes risk — the risk of seeing the benefits and actually changing! That risk of actually changing does not come alone either. It comes with significant rewards. If challenge and opportunity are not enough, just the knowledge of another way of doing something, which either worked or did not work, provides for significant personal and/or professional growth.

The truth of the matter is there can be no advancement without experiencing change. But there can be change without experiencing advancement. It is this fact of nature that many folks dwell upon to help them justify their negative view of change.

●●●

Negative paradigms concerning change are unproductive for many reasons, not the least of which is that they create a "self-fulfilling prophecy." In a changing environment, it is very beneficial that people work together and share their ideas, information and skills. The synergy of effective teamwork, focused on the success of a new endeavor, will maximize the chance of positive results. How easy is working as a team if what we believe concerning change is negative and we believe the new is going to harm us in some way? When we start concerning ourselves with basic safety issues, we begin a downward slide on Maslow's much discussed hierarchy. We "circle the wagons" and watch out for our own hides — not the classic description of your basic team players. This lack of team play then reduces the chance of success. When the inevitable, less than desirable results occur, we shout from the mountain tops, "See I told you so!"

Not only does the negative belief concerning change have its own dictionary definition, it also carries its own acronym, the RC Factor. The Resistance to Change Factor should always be calculated when figuring effects of a proposed change. **People feel discomfort because it is easier to see what is going than to see what is coming**. Remember, we see only the past. The future is an unknown and that translates, for some, into "scary."

Let us not dwell on the negative any longer. Anyone wishing to internalize any more negative responses need just ask around. A person can always find someone to give an earful. One can easily find someone who suffers from what, Ashley Montagu, the anthropologist, calls "psycho-sclerosis" or a hardening of the categories.

When we are faced with change, before we behave in any way, we should call "time out" and analyze what we are choosing to believe. Where are we setting our remote control? Is that setting creating defensive or accepting feelings? We must not get discouraged if our initial reaction is negative. This reaction to the unknown is natural and has kept the human race alive for millions of years. The question becomes, "How appropriate is that negative reaction?" The belief we carry with us is our choice. **Why would we choose an inappropriate, negative, change belief and yet choose to live in an environment of constant change?**

● ● ●

One spring afternoon my wife and I were having a picnic lunch next to a mountain stream. This stream moved at approximately the speed limit for a stream filled with run-off from winter, high-country snows except at the place where it tumbled down a small depression in the river bed over some rocks. The result created a small, active waterfall.

As picturesque as the whole river was, flowing into and coming out of the waterfall, I couldn't take my eyes off the excitement and the energy caused by this otherwise calm water's passage over the diminishing levels of earth and random accumulation of rocks. The waterfall appeared to give the river new life.

In the "stream of our life" (Fans of sappy metaphors ought really to eat this one up!), don't we sometimes need the spontaneous chaos of the "waterfall" to fill us with this same kind of excitement and energy? Being like Old Man River and just "keepin' on rollin' along" may get us from one end of this life to the other through calm waters. But you have to wonder, "Is it worth all the rowing?"

Noel Tichy from the University of Michigan describes what he calls the "Boiled Frog Syndrome." He applies this to organizations that get too comfortable, that are just "rollin' along," but the syndrome is equally appropriate for individuals.

If one puts a frog into hot water, it will jump out. Put the frog into cool water and it will just sit there doing frog things. Then gradually heat the water. The water becomes so comfortable that the warmth saps the frog's strength. The frog "croaks" — boiled frog.

Change in nature is not a philosophical choice. It is a survival choice. Over time, we either grow or we die, and we cannot grow without change. Humans are the only organisms in nature who can voluntarily change. Therefore we have control over our intellectual and/or emotional growth and can grow just as far as our pain of change will let us. Alvin Toffler in his classic book, *Future Shock,* said that humans have a limited capacity for change. Toffler does not say what that limit is for the obvious reason that the limit differs for everyone. The question we must all ask ourselves is, "**Have we even come close to our limits?**"

● ● ●

As much as we complain and fight the very concept of change, we sometimes, to spice up life, to feel excited again, to grow, will bring change upon ourselves. Why do we do this?

Consider this "typical" American life:

From birth to five-years-old everything in our lives, from the time we get up (earlier than our parents would like) until the time we go to bed (later than our parents would like), is exciting and full of learning experiences. Then we go off to school, kindergarten first, where according to that very aware author, Robert Fulghum (See Suggested Reading.), we learn everything we need to know. Society does not fully subscribe to Fulghum's basic truth and sends us on to eight years of pre-high school. During these years we continue our discovery, both in and out of the classroom. Every day is a new learning experience. We spend the year before high school enjoying being a BPOC (Big Person On Campus) and also being a bit afraid of being the low person on the totem pole again next year.

Then we are in high school. In class we learn "school things"; outside of class.... Well, we do not have to go very deeply into that. Let us just say those are interesting times. We begin to relate to the opposite sex, get our driver's license (which may determine how well we relate to the opposite sex) and really get a handle on how to drive our parents crazy.

Then some go off to college (those who really had trouble picking things up in kindergarten) while others head for the wonderful world of work. New and exciting challenges all! Over these next few years we marry and have children (the preferred social order), certainly major learning experiences. We now each have a new spouse, new kids and a new job to keep us stimulated, challenged and excited. Before we know it, we're forty-plus-years-old and our spouse, kids and job are all "not new!" Our children are starting to treat us like we treated our parents and our spouses and jobs are not treating us at all. We realize that the last time we were excited was when Jimmy Carter became president and our biggest challenge is trying to win the Publishers'

Sweepstakes without subscribing to any magazines. As far as being stimulated, that is the sole responsibility of the second cup of coffee.

The preceding happens to all too many people. They spend a good portion of their lives looking for security, comfort and, in a word, safety. When they get it, they know something is missing and the pain of that loss drives them in a direction known by some as MID-LIFE CRISIS.

The American life as just discussed is set to ensure the above scenario happens by providing the challenge and excitement of learning new things through the planned progression of schools and work, but **growth will stop — unless we choose to bring excitement and challenges back into our lives**. This is now our responsibility, not society's.

This desire to bring change into our lives is the reason a person who could have been a yuppie poster child trades in his forty-year-old spouse for two twenties, buys a pick-up truck and heads off to a cabin in the mountains to write the great American novel.

Introducing change to stimulate growth is not an activity reserved only for individuals. Organizations need change also. A CEO of a major U.S. corporation attested to this by saying, **"We reorganize for good business reasons. One of the good business reasons is that we haven't reorganized for awhile."**

LIFE CYCLE

Change, simply stated, is that something which was something is now something else. The reason it did not stay the something it was is because of the second law of thermodynamics (entropy). Entropy means that systems tend to break down over time. They break down to the extent that the energy needed to maintain systems exceeds the initial energy needed to start them. **Entropy applies to all systems, which is why systems either grow or die.**

To illustrate this essential process of change we will use a standard life cycle diagram.

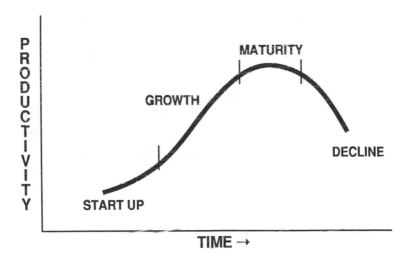

An example of how the life cycle works in a business:

Once there was a young man who wanted to go into business for himself. He wanted the challenge of starting his own business and the satisfaction of doing something he believed in which would also benefit others. So he opened a peanut butter pizza restaurant.

If we were able to observe, unnoticed, each phase of this "interesting," new business, following is what we might see.

START UP —— high energy, curious, creative, innovative workers. Distinguishing the boss from the employees is hard. Everybody is up to his elbows in pizza dough when not out delivering pizzas, distributing circulars or waiting on tables. The pluses of working in a start-up operation are the excitement and the challenge. The downside is the new venture may not succeed. The role of the employee in this phase is to take risks, to handle failures, to be creative and to be innovative. The role of the boss is to allow people to take risks, to treat failure as a learning experience and to reward creativity and innovation.

The boss's vision for the new venture and his ability to communicate excitement for the vision are critical in this stage. In a start-up phase, displays of hierarchical control such as large offices for management, reserved parking spaces and executive eating areas are rarely in evidence. The subjects of work hours, desks by the window and who has the corner office (or the office furthest from the boss) do not dominate the conversations. This phase takes time with productivity at a minimum.

GROWTH —— high productivity over less time and with less day to day excitement. The people work at a steady pace. Employees are generally less curious, creative or innovative. Those traits are not needed to the same degree as they were in the start-up phase. Creativity and innovation may even get in the way of smooth operations. Handbooks, policies and procedures are now in place and expected to be followed. After all, they have been proven to work. The employees now know how long to leave the pizza in the oven at 350 degrees without the peanut butter running all over. If employees start being innovative and creative, somebody will probably have to clean up after them. The role of an employee evolves into one of being a follower of rules and regulations. The boss's responsibility in this phase is to ensure that the workers follow those rules and regulations.

There are definite benefits in this phase. Activities have settled down. Tomorrow stands a good chance to be like yesterday. In other words, business is predictable, but, most important, it is more productive. With these benefits come the other side of the coin. Business is getting boring; the challenge has diminished and the excitement is increasingly found off the job. Different size offices for different levels of management begin to pop up. Those aggravating reserved parking spots multiply and the executive dining area begins to take shape. Employees' concerns with working hours and extra amenities in the work environment take up more management time. And, unlike the start-up phase, any discussion of vision or mission in the growth phase may tend to confuse and frustrate the workers.

MATURITY —— the growth phase, only more so. Not only is each day like the last one, but each month is like the last one. A complacency sets in and the only way the workers think they are contributing is doing what they did before, but harder. Turf issues seem to take on a life of their own. After all, if the organization begins to downsize, they want to have all the control they can with which to bargain. Office sizes, reserved parking places and executive dining areas are now critical. Employees' and management's roles are the same as in the growth phase: the employees follow the rules and management ensures they do. Maturity, like growth, can be either comfortable or boring. But one sure thing, maturity will not last forever.

DECLINE —— rapid loss of productivity over a relatively short period. Vision is completely lost, or at the least, misplaced. Blame and denial run rampant; résumés get updated; networking increases and trucks back up to the loading dock dropping off barrels of industrial strength Maalox, while simultaneously loading up with "outplaced" personnel. All in all, a sad end for our peanut butter pizza restaurant empire. But maybe it did not have to end that way. Entropy was allowed to happen. More energy was needed to keep the business going than the energy needed to start the business anew. So why not restart the business?

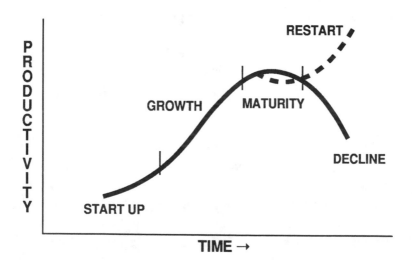

Knowing when to restart a business is tricky. As shown in the illustration, the restart phase consumes time while not being very productive. An organization does not want to get into restart too early in the maturity phase and thereby reduce productivity. Neither does an organization want to enter restart too late by being too far into decline, creating the same undesirable result.

Assuming the timing is on target, the following depicts what goes on in the restart phase.

RESTART —— Highly energetic, curious, creative, innovative workers. Hard to tell the difference between workers and the bosses — sound familiar? Restart has the same characteristics outlined in the start-up phase. Restart is another start up but on a higher level and with other peculiarities thrown in. Those peculiarities make restart challenging.

If the young entrepreneur becomes successful, he will need to do something or competition from bigger and better financed organizations may put him out of business. So he calls all of his people together and tells them while they have been highly successful just selling peanut butter pizzas, he is going to add a new product to the menu. He is going to add tuna and guacamole sandwiches (or open additional locations, add/eliminate certain business functions, restructure reporting responsibility, etc.).

What do you think the employees might say? "What's going on around here. We just figured out how to make a profit and now you are changing everything." "Why can't you just leave things the way they are!"

This brings us to what restart has that start up does not have — history. Is that fact good news or bad news? Yes. Restart begins with experience. That is the good news. But if we are "stuck," if that experience holds us back from the challenges of tomorrow by getting us all tangled up with the routines and thought processes of yesterday, then history is definitely the bad news. Restart may seem like, as Yogi Berra said, **"Deja vu all over again."**

In reality restart is not the same as start up. It may be the same change in form but it is being implemented in a different time, with its inherent different set of circumstances. While the acts we are performing are the same, the conditions surrounding the acts never are. We could put a stick into a stream at exactly the same spot everyday for the rest of our lives and not touch the same water. If nothing else, during restart we are older and wiser, or at least older!

Another trait of restart is that companies do not as a general rule terminate all their employees and hire new ones when they go into a restart mode. The people required to make restart work are the same ones working there during growth and maturity stages. These employees bring with them the good and bad news of history. More important, they carry forward the reward structure prevalent in their last phase. The rewards in maturity and growth were distributed for following the rules, while the required behavior in restart, as in start up, is to be a creative, innovative risk-taker! See any opportunities disguised as problems?

Consider desired manager behaviors during restart. Many managers in business today learned to be managers from their managers who learned from theirs and so on. Given the length of time most of our older companies have been in business, a good bet is that many of today's managers learned to be managers in either a growth or a mature environment. In those phases the manager's primary responsibility was to keep people following the rules as defined in well-established policies and procedures and to view with concern those employees who tested the boundaries of their jobs. These are the same managers who in a restart organization are being asked to encourage and reward creative, innovative risk-takers! See any additional "opportunities?"

Restart, as in start up, relies on a well articulated vision/ mission to provide its energy and focus. Old mission statements are dug out of the file drawer marked "M," dusted off and reworked to more accurately reflect the future. Or, as is most often the case, entirely new ones are prepared. As sure as potential professional baseball strikes are a sign of spring, the discussion and development of vision/mission statements by organizations are sure signs of a start-up or a restart operation.

The symbols of power in the organization, i.e. big offices, reserved parking spaces and the like are not a top priority in restart but they do still exist. Symbols are part of the history and, for those employees still "unclear on the concept," are hard to give up. The excitement and challenge of the restart phase is every bit as strong as in start up. So is the potential that the new direction may not be the right direction. The core substance of the growth and maturity phases is the stability provided, whereas the core substance of start up and restart is our old friend, change.

As exciting as the restart and start-up phases may appear to some people, remember these phases take time and the time they take is not very productive in the attainment of corporate objectives. While start up and restart are required phases of a renewing life cycle, the speed with which an organization enters and exits these low productivity phases may well determine organizational success or failure.

The example of a small business was used to illustrate the life cycle curve , but the process is also applicable to larger organizations (Ask A T & T, General Motors, DuPont, etc.). Also the life cycle curve can be used to display an individual's life. If we don't give ourselves a jump start, or more technically called a restart, we will be as dead as peanut butter pizza without tuna and guacamole.

PASSAGE

The saying that a person cannot reach second base without taking his foot off first is valid. That creates a great mental picture of a person stretching like a wishbone on a Thanksgiving turkey trying to occupy both bases. This image would be more humorous if so many people were not doing that very activity, not physically, hopefully, but certainly emotionally. Some individuals do not want to give up the safety of what is known for the uncertainty of the future. The fact is once reaching second base, this will be the "safe place" and third base will scare the "beegeebers" out of the runner. **Maybe the destination of our trip does not cause fear, as much as the trip itself**. When we are in no man's land between the bases, we are in "passage." We are in that place in which we do not have the security of the old nor do we have the excitement of the new.

Because of our concern about this passage, from what was to what will be, negative beliefs about change tend to surface. During this time we feel most vulnerable.

A personal example of feeling physically vulnerable during a passage came when I was taking karate lessons. Before attending the first session, if some guy had tried to hit me with his right fist, I would have, hopefully, blocked him with my left arm. That move is purely instinctive with most people. The only act that is more instinctive would be utilizing that very effective combination of running, screaming and hiding. But I was taught a "new and better" way to fend off a potential attacker. My instructor, Alex, said to do just the opposite. (And he should know. He was the owner of Karate-R-Us.) If anyone threw a right fist, I should, first, stay in the area and then block the blow with, of all things, my RIGHT hand! That was a "change." When thinking about it, the move made sense. By blocking the blow with the same arm the attacker was using, I was immediately out of harm's way. Also I had a great shot at the exposed ribs of anyone so foolish as to attack a trained killer such as Tom Payne.

So the old way was to use the opposite arm to block a blow. The new way was to use the same arm. I believed I could hold my own if, when necessary, I were to use instinctively either the old or the new way. But if anyone were to come at me during the passage from old to new, that time when the old way had been pretty well purged from my instincts and I had not yet incorporated the new way into my defensive arsenal, the attacker could, as they say,

"Have had his way with me."

While this story deals with the perils of physical passage, the same point holds true for emotional passage. It can be a scary time because, "It isn't what it used to be. It's not what it's going to be and I don't know what the heck it is now!" In the karate example I can take a real punch in the nose during passage; while emotionally, during change, I may take a good punch in the ego. The quicker we get through passage in our lives, the less bloodied we will be. **The quicker we get our coworkers and ourselves through passage, the quicker we can get back to the business of business.**

●●●

"Everybody's gotta be someplace." This basic truism tells us a little bit about where we and our coworkers may be in the change process — someplace. Having the whole team in exactly the same place on their trip from the old, through passage, to the new is desirable, but, in most cases, "synchronicity" is just wishful thinking. **Our responsibility during change is to accept wherever people are on the journey and to provide the support needed to move safely to the next step.** CAUTION: If we do not accept where a person is, that act will shut off communications. Emotions will be hidden in an abundance of malicious obedience, and disaster will be waiting around the corner.

Obviously passage between the old and the new is an essential step, but unfortunately some managers do not view passage as a manageable element and so passage is ignored. "The old is gone, long live the new!" is the battle cry of those soon to be confused by change. Two points concerning passage:

1) Passage needs to be managed.

2) Time of passage differs among people.

1) <u>Passage needs to be managed</u>.

Since passage is a finite period, something needs to be done to fill that time. What do employees in a changing organization most want from their managers during passage?

COMMUNICATION: "Just tell me what in the heck is going on so I can make needed decisions based on my personal and business objectives."

UNDERSTANDING: "Recognize what my rational and emotional concerns are. Don't rush me."

BEHAVIORS: "What do I have to do in the new environment to be successful?"

ROLE MODEL: "Boss, you look about ready to fall apart and you're telling me everything is all right!"

All of these wants are satisfied in a work relationship based on **mutual trust**. Unfortunately mutual trust is not a condition that is running rampant down the hallways of corporate America during periods of change. If mutual trust did not exist in the old environment, it may be able to be developed over time in the new, but you can bet your assets that it will not flourish during passage.

Managers can engage in open communications with their people, tell them that they understand what they are going through and outline all of the skills necessary to succeed in the new environment. A manager can walk around acting like "Mr. or Ms. Change," a super hero from whom people can derive courage. In other words a manager can do those activities that are needed and wanted at this time, but **without mutual trust, what is the point?**

Maybe this lack of mutual trust is why passage is not always managed effectively. The basic ingredient is missing. Does that mean that if mutual trust is a quart low in their work units, managers should give up trying to manage during passage? No, but they should not be too disappointed if managing passage does not work. Why should it? At the time workers are experiencing mental and maybe even physical trauma, the person who is there to help them through the tough times is someone they would not even put on their Christmas card list if they didn't think they had to!

So what should managers do? Get started developing trust in their work units right now. This might be only of minimal help during the current passage from the old to the new, but if the past serves as any indication of what is to come, another change series will be coming along soon.

Trust has to be earned with most people. This approach to human interactions is unfortunate. Too bad we cannot start with trust and proceed to "distrust," if that is warranted. Since initial trust is not the normal course of events in adult life, some time will be spent earning the trust of anyone who works with us. It is said that everyone, no matter how close to the boss she may be, is afraid of the boss to some degree or another. This cautious relationship does not quickly breed trust. Therefore managers must earn the trust of their subordinates. (SUBordinate sounds like subhuman. Maybe terms like that set up we/they manager/employee trust relationships.)

To earn the trust of another person, we must be real. To be real, in the sense meant here, is to have harmony between our mental and physical game, i.e. to have integrity between what is believed and what is done. If managers, do not believe their responsibility is to provide open communications, to "be there" for team mates during tough times, to spell out the new skills and/or to be role models, then they should not do it. If managers attempt to play that physical game when it is not in sync with their mental game (pretending), they will increase their stress and come across as phony and reinforce the thought, "Managers are not to be trusted." **A manager should not perform behaviors if she does not believe in them!** A suggestion would be either to find a job in an organization that is more stable, or to reframe beliefs concerning manager/employee relations during the change process.

●●●

Since we were emotional people before we were rational people, our first response to a proposed change will be most basic. How does it feel in our gut?

When helping people through change, consider the intensity of their emotional responses. Unfortunately the emotional issues are not often addressed. That is the result of a history in most corporate cultures, of only acknowledging the rational response.

Looking at an example: A typical conversation between a manager and an employee over consolidation of two departments might center around the employee's concern over how he will process the form PEC 1034 (affectionately known to all as the "Peck ten thirty-four") now that the department receiving the form no longer exists. The employee might go to great lengths to explain the difficulty this obviously blatant error will cause in product distribution and the resultant customer dissatisfaction.

If the truth be known (A sharp, empathic manager will know and act on the truth.), the employee is scared to death. The processing of the PEC 1034 is seventy-five percent of the employee's job description and the rumor is that part of this consolidation might include a dose of downsizing!

How far would people get in your organization saying they were afraid?

Dealing with the rational issues, rather than the emotional, concerning change is easier and usually quicker. That is why, in some instances, the rational is dealt with and the emotional is excluded. Dealing with the rational is generally easier and quicker (not to mention more comfortable), and time is the last thing workers feel they have in abundant supply during periods of drastic change.

Chapter 12 —— Change

A person has to be very clear as to what are the important elements of a successful change. Is it more important to get all the desks moved and the telephones installed in the new location on time? Or is it more important to have the people associated with the change be comfortable with it and willing to put their total effort into a successful beginning?

During periods of accelerated change, people have little time to spare, so it is important that the time is spent on the elements of the change that can most ensure its success, not necessarily on the elements that can be handled, easily, quickly and with the most comfort.

●●●

"How" we do things tends to change at a greater clip than "why" we do things. For example, a child, whose parents move to another home, may have to change schools. The change in schools brings with it a change in friends, enemies, (She had just figured out the difference in the last school.) teachers, physical surroundings, school bus routes and all those other elements that go into getting an education. But getting an education itself did not change. The "substance," obtaining an education, did not change. What changed was the "form," i.e. those components that went into getting an education.

In our work units, the substance is why we are in operation in the first place, to make a profit by solving customer problems. The form is how customer problems are solved. It is how we are organized, how many people do what jobs, how many layers of management are in place, how people are trained, etc. When thinking about it, **the substance of our lives changes little**.

Research shows that when a job changes as little as fifteen to twenty percent, the worker believes the whole job has changed. Now, of course, the form is changing constantly, but that should be acceptable because the purpose of the form is to aid us in accomplishing the substance. Accomplishing the substance is what we are all about. We must be always on the lookout for more effective forms to accomplish our substance. **If people focus on the substance (purpose/mission) of their personal and professional lives, due to the relative permanence of substance, there will be less churning, less change and less stress**.

To recap the first point, **passage needs to be managed through communications, understanding, behaviors and role modeling, all accomplished in an environment of mutual trust**.

2) <u>Time of passage differs among people.</u>

Employees bring to the workplace differing beliefs concerning change in general, and their own chance of success in the new environment, in particular.

People in your work unit may hold any one of the following beliefs. You may have coworkers who believe they are:

■ Doing well in the current environment/will do well in the new environment.

- Doing well in the current environment/not sure about the new environment.
- Doing well in the current environment/will do poorly in the new environment.
- Doing O.K. in the current environment/will do better in the new environment.
- Doing O.K. in the current environment/will do O.K. in the new environment.
- Doing O.K. in the current environment/will do poorly in the new environment.
- Doing poorly in the current environment/will do well in the new environment.
- Doing poorly in the current environment/will do O.K. in the new environment.
- Doing poorly in the current environment/will do poorly in the new environment.

Then of course, we have those who do not want the apple cart upset for many, nonjob related reasons.

The length of the passage is directly related to what the employee believes about his chance of success in the new venture. If a person is doing poorly in his job as it is currently structured and he sees the change as allowing his skills to be maximized, why would the individual choose to languish in the passage stage? Whereas if someone believes the opposite to be true, she would hang on to the old as long as possible, be dragged kicking and screaming into the passage stage and stay there until it appeared safe to come out. The manager's and coworkers' jobs are to intervene and to help create the environment where the worker will feel safe emerging into the "brave new world."

What does a person need to do to create this safe environment for himself and others? Specific action activities are available in Chapter Seventeen. To review some of the basics of managing passage in an environment of mutual trust:

■ Encourage an environment of open communications.

■ Help develop an environment of empathy by attempting to understand what coworkers are going through.

■ Support an environment of learning and teaching if necessary.

■ Provide a positive change role model.

■ Recognize time of passage differs among people.

●●●

The Chinese word for change contains two characters, one stands for danger and the other for opportunity. Which ever of these two characters is chosen with our remote controls will determine the effectiveness of our results and directly influence the quality of our lives.

It is not whether change happens or does not happen, what we choose to believe about change happening gives us control. Our ability to effectively manage change depends on what we perceive to be the consequence of the change. Do we view change as an opportunity for growth or do we focus on the danger of failure?

13

FAILURE: A BENEFIT OF EMPOWERMENT

Empower: To enable or permit. Empowerment is a popular word and concept from the corporate board room to the sanitation engineer's clooct, and no wonder, with all the downsizing/rightsizing going on! Somebody has to do the work!

In the interviews conducted for this book, at no time did anyone say, "Yes, they reduced our organization by two layers, and those two layers took all of their work with them." The truth is in the short run (however long that may be), the structure of the old organization, which was created and existed on certain policies and procedures, will roll merrily along as if the two layers were still available to do the work generated. This is the corporate version of the **"Phantom Limb"** syndrome.

People who have lost a limb sometimes feel sensation in the lost limb. They feel as if the limb is still operational. **Organizations may feel their lost layers are still operational and keep feeding work to the lost layers**.

Here lies the necessity for and the concerns with empowerment. Management needs people to take on extra and, many times, unfamiliar tasks (Note "The Fifty-Two.") which may lead to failure. The people who are asked to take on new and unfamiliar tasks may see failure as being punished to a significantly greater degree by the organization than achievement is rewarded. Therefore the concept of empowerment in these organizations holds little allure to the employee.

What we choose to believe about failure makes a dramatic impact on all aspects of our business and personal lives. The reason we are specifically addressing empowerment in this chapter on failure is because the need to "empower, to be empowered or to request empowerment if not offered" emerged very clearly in "The Fifty-Two."

Since **empowerment will not work without a personal acceptance and a corporate culture endorsement of the benefits of failure, our time may be best spent by examining failure in the context of empowerment**. The potential for failure and belief about failure play an important part for both the "empowerer" and the "empoweree."

Betty, a fourth level manager, had, in the old days, four third level managers working directly for her. Betty believed the role of a manager to be one of high control. Performing in that mode brought her considerable past success and with four subordinates, exerting control was not only possible, control was desirable. What else would she do with her time?

Until the punishment of being a control manager outweighs the benefits, Betty will continue in her controlling ways. Through rightsizing, Betty now finds herself, due to the elimination of the third and many of the second layers of management, with six first level supervisors and five nonmanagement positions as direct reports. If Betty continues her controlling ways, she will be hauled off to the

State Home for Over-Controlling Managers. So, Betty's behaviors, out of necessity, will become less controlling. (Betty's belief concerning her role may not have changed to match her new behaviors, in which case, as was discussed in Chapter Nine on stress, Betty will not be a happy camper.)

However, Betty's role is not the main issue when it comes to empowerment. Yes, managers have to give up control in order for empowerment to work but that release of power is relatively easy considering:

■ Managers do not have control anyway. If a manager quit her job and all of the workers stayed on the job, how much of the required work would get done? (Some people have said that 110 percent of the work would get done, which in itself tells something.) What if all the employees quit, leaving only the manager to attain the results? What percent of the work would get done? **Managers need their employees more than the employees need the manager**.

What would happen if the employees adopted a "malicious obedience" stance and only did exactly what the manager told them to do or what was written in job descriptions, company policies, procedures and handbooks? A definite possibility with an over-controlling manager!

Consider that insightful quote from Peter Drucker, "**Most of what we call management consists of making it difficult for people to get their work done.**" Managers who over-control use their time unproductively and make it difficult for their people to get their work done.

■ By the sheer number of employees compared to management, especially after rightsizing, the manager must begin at least the behavioral aspects of empowerment to survive. To attempt controlling more than five to eight people would be very difficult. **Putting authority in the hands of others, who knows how many one person could supervise**?

Managers, the Bettys of this world, because of basic survival instincts and the reality that they do not possess the control they think they do, have empowerment relatively easy — in contrast to the workers being empowered upon. Consider what life is like for the eleven people now reporting to Betty. Projects that Betty does not have the time and/or the knowledge to perform go to her "people." Betty's team members are now performing unfamiliar tasks which in the past were accomplished by one, two or three levels higher in the organization. An assumption that members of the current group might not accomplish these new tasks to the same degree of proficiency as the previous owners is reasonable. Therefore, as perceived through the eyes of the "empowerees," they are in a no-win situation — given tasks they will probably, to some degree or another "fail" in performing. Due to the "Phantom Limb" syndrome, their present tasks have not been curtailed, thereby reducing their current effectiveness. All this "failing" happens during a time of organizational downsizing (and it might be added, no additional pay). Where is the benefit of empowerment for the employee?

The benefits of empowerment for the employee are many: challenge, learning and growth being just a few. While these benefits are significant, they will never be realized without overcoming the self-established road-blocks we have been discussing. We have looked at the roadblock of change itself. Now we will look at the road-block of the fear of failure. **Consider how much easier it would be for an employee and the organization to enjoy the benefits of empowerment if the fear of failure did not exist**. Time to take our remote controls and search around for other ways to view the concept of failure.

●●●

What is the difference between the failure that causes people to commit suicide and the failure that causes people to double over in laughter? It must not be so much the concept of failure itself as how personally we take it; how the failure affects our self-worth; how it triggers the belief that we might not be as important as we think we are.

Our relationship to failure is based on what we choose to believe concerning failure. We are the only ones who determine if we fail, because we are the only ones who set up the expectations for the outcome. People with limiting beliefs give that control to others. They allow someone else's opinion of how acts should have been completed to determine their successes or failures, and their worth as employees or maybe even their worth as a human beings. That is too much control to give away.

A winner does not accept the concept of failure and that is all failure is, a concept. If there was not anything like failure, how would we know when we have succeeded? Failure gives meaning to success. Consider how fragile a concept failure is.

A salesperson sat in the office one day and made fifty cold calls to show the newer salespeople how to do it and did not get any appointments. Her coworkers were so impressed they took her out to dinner to celebrate her perseverance. She "failed" fifty times. How does she feel?

The concept of failure does not disturb people. It is the consequence of failure that disturbs people. What is the consequence of failure but an event on which we can place any belief we choose? Therefore **we have control over failure because we control what we believe about the consequences of failure**.

Think about the significance of that statement. We have control over what we believe concerning the consequence of failure and we can choose beliefs that will reduce the negative consequences of failure. And the negative consequences are what we fear.

What would you be doing right now if you did not believe there would be negative consequences if you failed?

What results in your business or personal life would be different if you did not choose to buy in on the negative beliefs concerning failure? Are we really stretching ourselves or are we living out our limitations through consequences we have imposed? We have all heard, "Don't bite off more than you can chew." How do we know the limits of our coworkers until they have been allowed to exceed their limits? How would we know how much we can chew until we have bitten off too much? Are we really trying to tiptoe through life to make it safely to death?

●●●

Failure is not given nearly the credit it deserves. Almost everything we know as adults had to be learned through failure. Think of yourself as a very young child just learning how to walk. Mommy's got you under the arms pointing you in the general direction of dear old dad who is shaking his car keys and babbling liko an escapee from the Home for the Torminally Proud (which is just up the street from the State Home for Over-Controlling Managers). Mom lets you go and you take off like you've got your knees on backwards. Two steps and you're down. Mom comes to the rescue and hauls you to your feet. Three steps and you're down. Mom's no quitter. You're up and down again. Sound familiar? At anytime during that learning experience, do you ever remember saying, "That's it. This is too embarrassing. Here I fell down five times in front of the two people I care most about in this world. As a matter of fact, they are the only two people I know in this world. My folks would like me to be in sports. Maybe they can just roll me in the swimming pool. Of course I'm such a failure I'd probably sink to the bottom like I was wearing lead diapers."

No, you just kept "failing" until you got it right. But at some chronological age many people decide they are too old to fail and it is then they begin to limit learning. Failure teaches as surely as success, but differently.

Do not worry about repeating errors because our brains, if left alone, will remember past successes and forget past failures. For example, in learning a new skill, like shooting free throws for basketball, the first time you tried it from the official free throw line, you might have made one basket out of ten. Hopefully improvement occurred and you started hitting two, then three and so on.

If our minds did not remember past successes and forget past failures, we would get worse at new skills because we failed more often than we succeeded. We would become a master at missing free throws because that is what we practiced the most.

BENEFITS TO FAILURE

Looking at some other stations that successful people choose to punch up on their remote controls:

■ Failure does not exist. It is only an experience that was less than anticipated. Everything we do has an outcome. If the outcome was what was expected or more — no failure. If the outcome was less than was expected — failure. The difference between success and failure is expectation. So failure teaches what to expect. **The number one benefit of failure is the learning experience, just another way of doing things**. When successful people have an experience that was less than anticipated, they will ask themselves, "What did I learn?" Consider on every occasion where you have an experience less than anticipated asking yourself, "What did I learn?" It is very critical that the question is phrased just that way, "What did I learn?" The temptation to ask, "Why have I failed?" is strong. Bad question! Following is a story to explain why.

As a young lad, Murray had troubles with math in school. He developed almost terminal math anxiety as a result of having to sit in the "dumb row" during arithmetic and listen to everyone laugh at his answers. (To the question "What is 28 plus 15?"; Murray once answered, "Columbus." This didn't help matters.) Externally Murray was being told he was very poor at math, that he seemed incapable of concentrating and that maybe he should invest in the most expensive calculator he could find. Murray was told he was going to need all the help he could get.

Everything externally introduced, Murray reinforced internally through negative self-talk. With that baggage, Murray entered high school. His negative belief concerning his math capability was even made worse, if possible, when he began studying Algebra. Algebra was very confusing to Murray because the teacher kept asking him what "x" stood for and as soon as he had figured it out, the teacher would change it. Murray reinforced his negative beliefs by complaining that he took basic algebra twice and still did not know what "x" stood for! College, believe it or not, was even worse.

With that background, Murray finds himself in the position of being "empowered" to do his work unit's budget, a task previously performed by his "outplaced" boss. No surprise to Murray, he prepares the budget incorrectly, or in other words Murray "fails." What do you think his answer would be to the question, "Why did I fail?" He would probably answer, "Because I've got the brains of a stalk of celery," a belief which may limit him in future mathematical endeavors. Whereas with the question, "What did I learn?" his answer may be anything from, "Never do those budgets again," to actually analyzing the budget process to find his mistake. **"Why did I fail?" leads to dwelling on the nega-**

tive. "What have I learned?" leads to growth.

■ Another benefit to failure can be found in a quote by the philosopher, Friedrich Nietzsche, **"Anything that doesn't kill me makes me stronger."** A person is tougher after a "less-than-anticipated experience." If people do a reality check, they would see that failure is more common than success.

We are in a giant numbers game, and **if the people in an organization are growing at all, they are going to fail more often than they succeed** — and that is O.K.

As Tom Peters says in his book, *Thriving on Chaos*:

> No issue is as important to tomorrow's manager as failure. We need more of it, lots more. The logic is simple:
>
> 1) We must innovate, in every department, faster.
>
> 2) Innovation obviously means dealing with the new, i.e. the untested.
>
> 3) Uncertainty is rising.
>
> 4) Complexity is rising.
>
> 5) Uncertainty is only removed and complexity dealt with by action.
>
> 6) To act on the new in the face of increasing complexity yields failure.

7) To act speedily ensures yielding speedy failure.

8) Rx for speedy innovation: more failure, faster.

9) Rx for dramatically speeded up innovation: dramatically increased rates and amounts of failure.

There are an almost irreducible number of failures associated with launching anything new. For heaven's sake, hurry up and get them over with.

Rocky Marciano said, "**It's not so important how often you get knocked down. It's how often you get up that counts.**" Think about that. People getting up one more time than they are knocked down, are standing at the end.

Decca records was still standing even though in 1962 they turned down the Beatles with the statement, "We don't like their sound. Groups of guitarists are on the way out."

How much do they pay a professional baseball player for failing seven out of ten times at bat?

Abe Lincoln was defeated thirteen out of sixteen times he tried for public office.

Van Gogh sold only one painting in his entire lifetime and that was to his brother!

The list of people and organizations who have tried, failed and come back could fill this entire book. It is not that failure happens (One half the people playing racquetball fail to win.), it is what we choose to believe about failure that will affect our results and our quality of life.

Many people and organizations fail simply because they give up before they succeed. Vince Lombardi was once asked why he lost a game. Vince said, **"We don't lose. Just sometimes the clock runs out too soon."**

In contrast to Vince's belief concerning perseverance was the attitude of Charles Duell, director of the U.S. Patent Office in 1899, who wanted to close down the office because as he said, "Everything that can be invented has been invented."

What do you think of the poor soul who was a researcher for a soft drink company and quit his research after he developed "6 Up"?

■ Last, **failure helps us develop a sense of humor**. Our strength as humans is our ability to laugh at ourselves. Our weakness is we have to do it so often. For example, on my first date at the movies, we sat down and I asked if she wanted some popcorn. Unfortunately, she did. Exiting into the aisle, my previous years of Catholic education hit me all at once and I genuflected in the middle of the theater. Another fact successful people know about failures is failures are time sensitive. The longer ago they happened, the funnier the failures are.

●●●

Empowerment, which can be a natural outgrowth of an organization becoming "lean and mean," will not work

without the ability of members of the organization to accept failure. Individuals in an organization may find it hard to accept the benefits of failure if they feel the organization is only giving lip service to the organization's stated desire for risk-takers in the ranks. Therefore the organization, which is all of us, must alter its chosen response to "outcomes that were less than expected to be." We must view the consequences of failures as: learning experiences necessary to get us where wo need tu be; a numbers game; past events good for a few laughs; and <u>not</u> as a potential loss of our job (or other perceived security). Let us move on to the subject of security, where it is and who has it.

14

SECURITY: WE CAN'T LOSE WHAT WE NEVER HAD

In the 1987 movie, *Mannequin*, a woman asks her often unemployed boyfriend, "Did you lose your job?" He answers, "No, I know just where it is and somebody else has it." People reframing their beliefs about job security in those terms are really gaining control.

This area of security is where many people tend to give up most of their control. Employees may get frustrated because they feel there was some kind of a "contract" entered into when they joined the organization. They think this loosely stated contract implies the employee would give up a certain amount of independence and in return would receive security. Therefore they perceive their security to be in the hands of the organization they work for, or in the case of personal relationships, in the person they live with, or perhaps both. "If I were to get fired, I don't know what I would do." "If she left me, I couldn't go on." Considering in the United States at least fifty-one percent of the new marriages will end in divorce (One hundred percent end in death.) and companies are reducing ranks by the thousands each year, people need to figure out how to react. A strong suggestion would be to reframe limiting beliefs concerning the source of individual security into beliefs more consistent with reality.

Time to set our remote controls to the reality that there

will never be 100 percent security. Anyone can lose any job or any relationship on any given day for many different reasons. **Absolute security does not exist, only varying degrees of risk** and what security there is, is not external, but internal. We are in charge of our own security.

●●●

Robert Tucker and Denis Waitley in their book, *Winning the Innovation Game,* use the term, "**You, Inc.**" This says it all — incorporating oneself, not in the legal sense, but in the sense of personal empowerment.

When people go on a job interview, what are they selling but themselves? The résumé is the brochure for the person who is the product. How does that brochure look? Would we buy ourselves? What do we have to offer? What would we like to add? The Bureau of Labor Statistics states that the average American worker today will work for ten different employers, keep each job only three and a half years and change entire careers three times before retirement. Are you ready?

A "You Inc." person is one who can and does stand alone. "I, Edward E. Employee, will sell my services to the ever popular XYZ Company for as long as there is a mutual benefit. But if there comes a time where there is not, I'll anguish for a while, but I'll be O.K., because I am self-sufficient. I know where my security lies."

A person with a strong sense of where her security origi-nates will do a self-analysis to bring to light what she needs to attain a high degree of self-confidence, and go get it. She realizes that **job security does not lie in the organization but in the quality of one's work**.

People need to ask themselves how prepared are they to function outside of their current jobs. What skills are needed to be more marketable? Is more computer knowledge needed or more experience in budgeting, finance, marketing, long range planning, etc., to round out their strengths?

WILLING TO WALK?

Robert Waterman in his book, *The Renewal Factor,* states that **the only power individuals have over the organization is their "willingness to walk."** (As harsh as that sounds, that is also true of relationships.) If we are not willing to walk, we will not speak out on tough issues. And we will not be willing to walk unless we are confident in our ability to survive alone. The need for the approval of others is an expression of our dependence and creates the belief our survival is in someone else's hands. While this is not true, it is easy to see how that belief originated.

For the first six months of our lives, we had it pretty good. Yelling, screaming, kicking up a fuss got the whole world, as we knew it, mobilized to help us. After six months we started to hear a word that we hadn't heard before, the word was "no." We now started getting our actions curtailed. Not only that, they now wanted something in return for what we used to get for nothing. For example: "Give Daddy a smile, and I'll give you a bottle of milky-wilky." (It is a wonder we ever grew up to speak even half way intelligently.)

Then we began to believe that survival depended on the attention, approval and protection of others. So we developed gas and screwed up our faces. Father thought it was a smile and we got milk, but the damage was done, and dependency on something or someone outside of ourselves was reinforced.

When experiencing fear of loss of security, remember we came into this world alone. We will leave this world alone and we will provide the only real security that will ever exist for us on this earth. We are in charge. We are in control.

$40 MILLION LOTTERY

"If you won the $40 million lottery and chose to stay working for your current employer, would job security be an issue?" The answer to that question, when asked during workshops, is a resounding, "No." **The reason for that obvious response is the employees would not <u>have to work</u>. They would be working because they <u>wanted to</u>, a whole new frame of reference**. The same response occurs when people are asked if job stress or time management would be a problem if they hit the big jackpot. What does that tell us?

An interesting sequence of events — the boss overloads Conrad with work. Conrad now has a time management problem — how to get all this new work done plus satisfactorily completing his existing assignments. Conrad knows to the depths of his being there is no way he can meet the boss's deadline (negative stress). If Conrad were to be asked why he is feeling stressed, he would say if he does not finish all the work assigned to him, he would "fail" on his job and with corporate justice carried to its fullest, he would be fired. Supposing Conrad wins the lottery. He now does not care if he gets fired or stays on the job, dramatically reducing his negative stress. The boss comes up to him with new work. Conrad says, "Thanks, I'll do the best I can." And at quitting time he goes home whistling a happy tune. Was the workload causing the stress?

If the concern for security were not so strong, consider how dramatically negative stress could be reduced thereby increasing productivity in the corporate environment. Some organizations/managers are "shooting themselves in the foot" over this security issue by scaring the living hell out of employees with threats of reducing security through salary reduction, demotion or the ultimate horror, termination.

Do organizations consciously use fear as a motivational tool? Probably not, but because so many employees harbor a deeply seated, and sometimes not so deeply seated, fear of losing their security, perceived punishment has created intense organizational dependence on the part of the employee. Organizations, for expediency purposes, will "ride the horse in the direction it is going." Because of following the path of least resistance to getting jobs done in the short run, they will threaten security. When employees buy it, employees lose. We have met the enemy and it is us!

Consider an entire work force of employees who have won the $40 million dollar lottery. How would an organization motivate its employees if there were no fear of losing job security? There would be only one way, and that would be to provide for each person a work environment that is fulfilling and rewarding for its own sake. To provide such an environment, the organization needs to supply a clear vision/mission/purpose which for each employee has meaning, substance and depth. The organization would also provide options for growth through special assignments, training outside of specialized areas, assignments on interdepartmental project teams, etc. In essence, **organizations would be creating motivational environments necessary to keep those employees who <u>choose</u> to work rather than creating fear techniques for those employees who perceive they <u>have</u> to work**.

●●●

If we expect our organizations to work hard at creating the same environment for us as they would need to create for the lottery winner, we must choose to view our need for organizationally generated security in the same way as the instant millionaire. **As soon as each worker realizes that the only security that does exist is within the self and he prepares for and can visualize a future without his company, then the worker can truly choose to be a participating member of that organization.** When the majority of workers in corporate America are of this mind, we will witness a significant increase in corporate productivity and the greatest shift in organizational motivation patterns since the Emancipation Proclamation.

We are motivated by our organizations as we have taught our organizations to motivate us. Therefore we must reduce our dependence on the organization (reframe beliefs concerning the real source of security), if we are to have the creative, innovative, risk-taking and growth-oriented work environment so desired and so required in a changing business environment. In some ways that is as good as winning the lottery!

In the next chapter, you will be reading about the key to the mastery of change, to the acceptance of failure, and to the understanding of security.

SELF-ESTEEM: KEY TO THE MASTERY OF CHANGE

Was Alexander the Great self-confident? Probably he was, otherwise he would have called himself Alexander the Pretty Good! The key to self-confidence (opposite of self-doubt) lies in the ability to see ourselves as winners. Considering the odds of being born of a single mating are said to be over 300 million to one, we all started as winners.

Would someone who saw herself as a winner be bothered to the point of severe stress by change, by the thought of failure or by the risk of losing security? **The key to gaining mastery over change and its fallout of failure and security issues lies in what we think about ourselves**. How many of us, as young children, saw ourselves or our world as limited? When we were young, we imagined ourselves as limitless. Look how many kids thought they could be doctors and began practicing at a very early age.

When our education began, we learned what we could not do, and through our self-talk we reinforced our perceived limits. We have met the enemy and it is still us.

Where did some of our negative input originate? Shad Helmstetter in his book about self-talk, *What to Say When You Talk to Yourself,* quoted research that stated by the time a child reaches eighteen years of age, he will have heard the word "no" or "you can't" 148,000 times. (And that does not even count the times teenage boys hear those words from teenage girls.) The figure comes to about one and a half times every waking hour. A University of Iowa study determined the national average of criticism to praise from parents to children runs about twelve to one and eighteen to one for teachers to students. **What is the good of teaching our children if they are not taught a sense of their own personal worth**? The reality is the choice of deciding which of all the external input to let in, the eighteen criticisms or the one praise, is ours. It is our choice as to what we will believe about ourselves and our limits.

PROGRAMMING PERSONAL LIMITS

Since the individual's personal perception begins externally and is reinforced internally, reviewing the self-talk people use to program in their personal limits is important. We must watch for the following limiting words and phrases in our own vocabulary as well as in the vocabulary of our team members.

■ I can't.

"I can't" literally means impossible and if what we are using "I can't" with is literally impossible like the Chicago Cubs winning a World Series, then the phrase is appropriate.

But be careful, if Einstein had said, "I can't," "I can't because I flunked math in school," we would be missing a few good formulas.

If the Wright brothers had said, "We can't," "We can't because we're only bicycle mechanics," we would be missing the opportunity to have our luggage sent to towns thousands of miles from where we are.

If Jim Abbott had said, "I can't," "I can't play baseball because I only have one hand," we would have missed out on watching him win the prestigious Sullivan Award as the top amateur athlete in 1987. This award was won by a team player for the first time in fourteen years and the first time ever by a baseball player. To add to his accomplishments, he became the first rookie in the 1989 professional baseball season to win seven games.

In 1986, in Arlington Heights, Illinois, a thirteen-year-old girl came home with a bronze medal she had won in a national karate competition held that year in Atlanta, Georgia. Jennifer Malloy would not have come home with that medal if she had said, "I can't." "I can't compete in a karate competition, because just eleven days ago I underwent a ten and a half hour operation where doctors drilled holes in my skull to stop the growth of muscle cancer affecting my head and neck." If Jennifer had said "I can't," we would have missed a demonstration of karate that brought her four tenths of a point from the gold medal. We would have missed comments from the judges like, "Good balance, very good focus and good composure." We would have missed an excellent opportunity to know a person who was only as limited as she believed she was. **Limitations tend to be true in experience because they are believed rather than the reverse.** Jennifer Malloy died about eight months later, beating her cancer but losing to pneumonia. To use the word "losing" anywhere in a story about Jennifer Malloy simply does not track with her life.

Jennifer's mother eulogized her as a person who "inspired kids to do their best. Jennifer always said she wanted to show people that no matter what was wrong with you, you could still have fun and keep trying." Thirteen-years-old! The next time you or a member of your team are tempted to say "I can't," give Jennifer a thought.

■ Never

"Never," as used in "I never have been able to...," addresses perceived past limitations. If the past is at fault for what we are today and we do not believe we can change the past, we are doomed to stay the way we are.

■ It's not fair.

"It's not fair" carries with it an expectation that we are good people, therefore the world should treat us in the way we want to be treated. That is a little like expecting the bull not to attack us because we are vegetarians.

■ Have to

"Have to" is a particularly harmful phrase because our power of choice is reduced. Imagine sitting around the office talking to a friend and telling her about the power and control you have through the choices you make, and she asks you to tell her more. You say, "I'd like to stay and talk but I have to go back to my office and write performance appraisals."

Great control — you <u>want</u> to stay and yet you <u>have</u> to go. The reality is that you do not <u>have</u> to go. Think of the things you really and truly <u>have</u> to do. Death is about the only one.

Everything we do on this earth, including our reaction to change, is a choice, and that is the truth. We do not <u>have to</u>; we <u>choose to</u>. Our language customs make lying to ourselves and others easy. For example, telling a friend, "I'd like to talk to you but I have to go back to my office and write performance appraisals," is more socially acceptable than saying, "I'd like to talk to you but I choose to go back to my office and write performance appraisals." "Great, instead of talking to me, he would rather write appraisals which ranks just above a lower GI exam with most people. I now know where I stand."

If you were to draw a line and put "have to" on one end of the line and "want to" on the other, then place all the tasks you have scheduled for the day somewhere on that continuum and if you could do any task you wanted, which end of the line would you head for? **"Have to" creates resistance and takes away personal control. "Want to" and "choose to" create desire and return control. A self-confident person chooses to do everything he does.**

■ Should

"Should" (As used in "Upper management should tell us what is going on around here," and "My group should be excited about this move.") takes away its user's power. Should immobilizes the person in the present moment by requiring spending that present moment wishing events

were different from what they are. Anything that has happened should have happened; otherwise it would not have
happened! The event did happen and is over and done.
Rather than fussing and fuming over the irretrievable past,
use the present moment to put a structure into place so a
similar undesirable event does not happen again in the
future.

An interesting exercise: Think of a result in your life which
you want, i.e. I <u>want</u> to react positively toward change.
Then substitute for "want," "have to, should, or need to."
Such substitutions surely dampen a person's passion,
don't they? Now in place of "want," use "choose, desire or
can." How do those feel?

■ <u>Categorizing Phrases</u>

These are phrases like "I am...." How would you finish
that sentence? Was your answer positive or negative? Do
you hear yourself or team members saying any of the
following: "That's me!" "I've always been that way!" "I can't
help it." "That's just my nature." (Some people use them all
in one sentence. "That's me; I've always been that way; I
can't help it; it's just my nature.") These phrases can be
influential positive or negative forces because they reflect
beliefs. People find difficulty behaving the opposite of their
beliefs.

●●●

Limiting words and phrases are certainly reinforced and
given their emotion and energy internally through self-talk,
but as mentioned earlier they did not originate internally.

Chapter 15 —— Self-Esteem

The following is a personal example of some external input to a self-limiting belief system:

It was third down, two yards to go for a first down at our opponent's ten yard line. We (St. Patrick High School) were on a roll. I was playing fullback on that memorable Sunday afternoon. (The afternoon was memorable because we were on our way to a touchdown which could win the game for us, the first in three and a half years.) The coach called all the shots and sent in the halfback with the play the coach felt could get us a touchdown and salvage some degree of respectability, not to mention his job. The half-back joined us in the huddle and told us the play. The coach, in all his wisdom, had called my number. I was going to carry the ball. Just before we broke the huddle, the halfback leaned over to me and said, "The coach said that whatever you do, don't fumble." To this day, the ball has not been located, and I picked up the nickname "Cinderella" because I missed the ball.

While everybody else was going to psychology classes in college and learning that the subconscious mind does not focus on the opposite of an idea, my coach must have been taking double biology credits so he could boil twice as many frogs. To show how difficult focusing on the opposite of an idea is, try this little exercise: close your eyes for ten seconds and whatever you do, do not think of a football. What was the only thing you saw? Sure, a football, big as life. The subconscious mind does not focus on the opposite of an idea.

Golfers, do you ever say to yourself, "O.K. klutz, whatever you do, don't hit it in the water." Then you tee up an old ball just to make sure you never see it again.

We definitely need to program ourselves with positive, winning thoughts. Self-confident people do not fall into the trap of sabotage, either of themselves or of others. In the golf example, we sabotage ourselves. In the football example, I let others sabotage me.

Here is another example of how we let others mess with our self-confidence, and since I am already on the football coaches' blacklist, I might as well just keep on going.

When playing football in college, the coaches took movies of each game. (This was 1960 B.V. — Before Video.) They took movies to "help us become better players," and it worked in much the same way as the electric chair helps convicted murderers become better citizens.

I remember one game in particular. The camera focused in on an opposing player running around the end, and as luck would have it, yours truly was the only one between the runner and a sizable gain. I never had the quickest reflexes. As a matter of fact I was once hit by a car with a flat tire that was being pushed by two guys. (I really should have been able to react quicker because across the front of the car was written "Dodge.") Even so, I felt pretty good about myself and my abilities — until exposed to a little help from my coaches.

The camera was able to isolate just the runner and me. He faked; I bought it, put a great tackle on where he used to be and, in compliance with the law of gravity, settled in a cloud of dust. It was all natural turf in those days. The camera caught every agonizing moment of that play.

(Anybody who has ever played in a sport where movies or video tapes were taken by the coaching staff, knows what is coming.) At the next practice session, when the coach came to the part of the movie where the tackle was missed, he showed the play, rewound it, showed it again, rewound it, showed it again, and rewound it for what seemed like half of my life. All the time he was telling me, and anyone else who would listen, while also reinforcing my "failure" visually, what a lousy tackler I was. **Where does learning stop and damage to self-esteem begin**?

What had my coach accomplished? Since a person's subconscious mind believes everything imagined vividly and in detail, did I leave that room a better or a poorer tackler than when I went in? I had trouble putting one foot in front of the other while walking out of the meeting! Worse yet, how did I leave as a person? How was my self-confidence? I left that encounter with another human being, who had position power as a coach, internalizing the negative, giving emotion to my failure, and developing limitations that I did not bring into the meeting. Who benefitted?

Sure, the choice as to how to take the coach's criticism and my team mates' verbal shots was mine. The responsibility for my tackling results was mine. But at that age when someone you respect tells you that you are no good, it is tough. The worst part is that didn't have to be. I made some good tackles in that game. The coach could have as easily showed me making a proper tackle over and over. I would have left that practice with a visual picture of exactly how a good tackle looks, and with me doing it! Then when the missed tackle reared its ugly head on the screen, he could have used a couple of showings as a learning experience by asking, "If you had that tackle to do over again, what would you have done differently?" An opportunity to improve self-esteem and productivity was wasted.

Coaches, parents, work team members note: the power which our teams, our children, or our coworkers give us to help make them the best they can be cannot be underestimated. Give a break to those who look to you for guidance, either because they want to or because they have to. Make it easier for them to maximize their potential by emphasizing their strengths. Create the environment in which they can easily feel self-confident. Catch them doing things right and help them learn from those experiences that have not gone right.

We must focus on what we want to see happen, not on what we do not want to see happen. Saying "Don't be late with that report again this month," creates a negative focus. The person may then spend valuable work time concentrating on "not dropping the ball."

●●●

Change creates fertile ground for self-doubt with possible new skills to be learned (See "The Fifty-Two."), new people to be met, new physical surroundings to which to adjust, new management to work around, new customers to satisfy or all of the above. As discussed, people do not necessarily behave in accordance with reality, but behave in accordance with their perceptions of reality, their paradigms. **Whatever we can do to create the reality of competence for those with whom we are associated, the greater chance we will all have for success.**

One last thought to keep in mind regarding self-esteem! Western culture is basically a left-brained, problem-solving culture. We look for problems and attempt to solve them. That gets us to look for problems in other people and let them know about their faults, so either we or they can get them fixed. The reality is there is always somebody out there willing to tell us what is wrong with us — of course, for our own good. Our life on earth may not be long enough to see the negative criticism change. Not to hear some of our faults from others would be almost impossible, but we still have the power to set our remote controls. **We have the ability to choose what we will let in for ourselves and what we will see in others. We have the ability to see people as they can be, not necessarily as they are.**

We choose what to reinforce for ourselves through empowering self-talk such as "I can," "I choose to," and/or "I want to." We can also influence how team members see themselves by not tolerating negative words and phrases in the work unit. **Self-doubt exists right along with self-esteem — our choice.**

SECTION THREE

Practical Steps to Implementing Change

16

HOW TO USE THE "HOW TO" CHAPTERS

The title of this book, *From the Inside Out*, explains how successful change can occur on both a personal and organizational level. We have looked at how the individual can "from the inside" aid in his or her own success in a changing environment. Section Three will cover a wide variety of "outside" activities implementable by work group members, regardless of the job or title. These positive actions will increase the chances of personal, team and organizational success during periods of change. (If you currently are not a member of a work group, consider the personal value of many of the "How Tos.")

A major concern of workers during periods of dynamic change is that they might <u>fail</u> in the new environment. That failing may cause a perceived lack of <u>security</u> which could adversely affect their <u>self-esteem</u>. Since these roadblocks are so interconnected, you may find some "how tos" in each chapter to be slightly similar. You may find that a specific activity listed for establishing a positive climate for change may be more useful to you in creating an environment where it is acceptable to fail. Use the activity where it will do the most good.

Read each section to ensure exposure to the greatest number of options. Obviously not every activity will apply to every situation. Determine the listed activities that will have the most significant impact on your personal, team and organizational productivity. The next step, in order to establish an action plan, would be to process the selected activities through the Tactical Strategies Plan format explained in Chapter Twenty-One.

The activities in Section III are listed by chapters according to the "roadblock" but not in any particular sequence, order or priority within that category.

As stated, every idea will not be appropriate for every occasion. All are included because I believe in the approach stated by a successful east coast retailer, who said when asked about the size of his advertising budget, "I know fifty percent of my advertising budget isn't worth a damn. I just don't know which fifty percent." I would rather provide "overkill" and leave you inundated with new ideas than provide "underkill" and leave you wanting.

●●●

People today have the skills to do what needs to be done. Nothing new has to be added. The skills currently possessed need only to be taken out, dusted off and put to work. **People do not get paid for what they know, but for what they do with what they know**. As was mentioned earlier, knowledge is power, but only knowledge that is put to work is really power. A person may know everything there is to know about hang gliding but if the knowledge is not put to use, she will know exactly why she is plummeting to earth at hundreds of miles per hour, but so what?

Due to the general audience for a book of this nature,

and for the variety of ever-changing circumstances out in business land, these suggestions may not all be strictly classified as "behaviors" (measurable and observable). Some may be more accurately classified as attitudinal "how tos," but whenever possible, measurable and observable examples are provided. When you choose which activities are most appropriate to implement, please ensure that, for your unique situation, the activity is defined in specific behavioral terms.

A quote from Peter Drucker is appropriate at this point. **"Everything must degenerate into work if anything is to happen."** Nothing in this entire section will "happen" if you are not committed to implementing it! **Change does not take time only; it takes commitment** Save yourself some valuable time. If you are not committed to change and if you are not committed to do what it takes to alter change results, do not bother reading Section III. Spend your time more productively by reading something that will do you more good — like the want ads.

17

HOW TO ESTABLISH A POSITIVE CLIMATE FOR CHANGE

■ Treat change as the norm. "That's the way we do things around here." Norms in a work unit are like habits to an individual. Habits/norms can be very productive in utilizing time but can also be destructive, primarily because we perform habits without thinking. If our results are not what we desire, it is important that we think in order to know why. Long-term employees may have "forest for the trees" mind-sets. Consider asking a new team member to tell you both the positive and the negative norms she notices within the first month on the job, before the person becomes blinded by acculturation. **Is change in your work unit being treated as the norm or as the plague?**

■ Generate small changes daily. Be creative. Have Monday's meeting on Tuesday, or if you have nothing to cover, cancel the meeting completely. Discontinue some reports and/or reassign some minor job responsibilities, etc. Recognize the power of the Hawthorne Effect which, briefly stated, contends any nonthreatening change will improve morale and productivity. Small changes equal big results.

■ Stress the dangers of complacency and self-satisfaction. (Award the dreaded "Boiled Frog" trophy to those too comfortable in their jobs.) To paraphrase Peter Drucker, in this "Age of Discontinuity," the time to rethink technology and business strategies is precisely when they are working best. Attack tomorrow from a position of strength.

———

■ Submit suggestions for the next change just after the last change. This approach reinforces change as the norm, gets the people thinking in the longer term and involves others more deeply in the change process.

———

■ When interviewing for people to hire as members of the team, look for those who have succeeded in their past assignments, not in spite of change, but because of change. They say there are three kinds of people:

> Those who make things happen.
> Those who watch things happening.
> Those who don't know anything is happening at all.

Be sure you know with which of these people you are working.

———

■ Provide meaningful and relevant work immediately after change that uses the people's hard-earned and fiercely protected "old skills." Once an individual realizes that he does indeed have some transferable skills, the time involved in passage is reduced. As Alfred E. Neuman said, **"Just because everything has changed doesn't mean anything is different."**

———

■ Keep team members informed constantly about what is going on in the organization and how they are contributing. Change is not the time for "Mushroom Management." Over-informing is better than under-informing. Develop new and expanded methods of communications (meetings, newsletters, rumor hot-lines, etc.).

■ Provide team members the opportunity for true participation in team decisions through focus groups. The workers are the true experts; they are now, or will be soon,
performing the functions to make the new environment
productive. Subscribe to the corollary of the *Peter Principle*
that says, **"Decisions rise to the management level
where the person making the decision is least qualified
to do so."** Not to make use of all available points of view
during periods of change will only lengthen the overall
process and could tend to foster resistance from those
required to make the change work.

**Change results are inevitable. If we do not plan the re-
sults, somebody else will.** We might as well get the involved people planning from the beginning. People who
are involved in the process tend to be committed to the
results.

■ Communicate and work with the vision/mission so
people see the substance has not changed. Workers need
to understand that "why" they are working has not
changed. "How" they accomplish the "why" may have
changed. In today's environment the "how" will rarely
remain constant.

■ Become a learner — read, listen, watch, and act. We
then become a valuable resource for our team.

■ Ask to be moved around before you start to get stale.
While this churning may adversely affect productivity over
the short term, it contains many significant long-term benefits. Those employees least likely to cope during periods of

change are those folks most sheltered and isolated.

———

■ Provide constructive and immediate feedback, consistent with a team member's job maturity. Feedback is more than just letting people know how they are doing. It also deals with the results of the entire organization, the work group, etc.

Research studies have shown that as much as fifty percent of performance problems occurs as a result of a lack of feedback. This is a touchy area because you do not want to provide excessive corrective feedback, perceived as negative, to someone trying a new task. It could limit future attempts. As Mark Twain said, "The cat, having sat on a hot stove lid, will not sit upon a hot stove lid again. Nor upon a cold stove lid."

———

■ Strive for total commitment from the work group. They may not agree on 100 percent of the change, but it is vitally important to the success of the new endeavor to have total commitment. Because as they say, "**It is hard to cross a chasm in two small jumps.**"

———

■ Here is a technique that may work with those who are taking up an excessive amount of time with concern over change. Ask the person to:

> 1) Take five minutes and jot down her concerns on paper. (This step alone may eliminate the concern.)

> 2) Write about what is really bothering her and what she would like to see happen.

3) Write the first realistic and workable behavior required to obtain the desired result stated in step two.

After the person is finished writing, sit down and talk about what needs to be done. These discussions should be kept in a positive (How can we make this work?) mode. There is no benefit to legitimizing complainers.

The more a person is focusing on what is wrong with the new, the more he sits around "catastrophizing" and "awfulizing," the less he is focusing on how to fix the situation. If the person can not buy off on the change, it should be O.K. for the individual or the organization to request a transfer without having this request listed forever under "not a team player" in the "permanent record." Having someone on the team who cannot commit to the team's future is not of benefit to the individual or to the organization.

■ Review your interpersonal style. Is it appropriate? Is it working?

■ Accept wherever a coworker is emotionally during the change process. To want people to be someplace other than where they are, is an exercise in futility. There are better places to spend time then to wish people were not where they are. The FUD Factor (Fear, Uncertainty, Doubt) is real and must be acknowledged.

■ Be sensitive about which environment the worker feels the greatest loss during periods of change.

-physical (office space, equipment, etc.)
-social (coworkers, team spirit)
-psychological (support from boss and organization)
-intellectual (creative interactions with coworkers)

What can you or the organization do to reduce the negative impact of that loss?

———

■ Consider volunteering for less familiar tasks to facilitate learning.

———

■ Bring in someone to speak to your group who has had a successful experience going through the changes the group is now going through. Why should your group reinvent the wheel? Just think of how long it would take to learn everything we now know if we had to learn everything ourselves and could not rely on the experiences of others?

———

■ React with calm. After all, change is the norm in your operation, isn't it?

———

■ Update your résumé and consider encouraging coworkers to do the same. This activity increases workers' feelings of control. While having everyone with updated résumés may appear harmful to the organization, just the opposite is likely to occur. The knowledge that a person has something to offer outside of her organization is an empowering piece of news and frees the individual to be creative and to take risks. Both characteristics are needed in a changing environment.

———

■ Provide team members with new knowledge and a full range of responsibilities so they will be able to more effectively cope with both the concept and the reality of change. The person is better off because he now has less fear of the unknown because less is unknown. The organization has a more well-rounded employee.

■ Discourage, to a significant degree, negative talk concerning change. Team members should, of course, be allowed to communicate their feelings but the conversation must be directed to how the perceived problems can be overcome. Sitting around creating a "whine list" is time-consuming and a good bet is it will result in negative productivity.

■ Ask to be assigned to teams with others you do not know (other work groups, branches, departments). This technique provides cross learning and may aid in increasing self-confidence to handle change.

■ Stay away from doing jobs during change that can be done by machines. Concentrate on those activities, such as communicating, problem-solving, empathizing, conflict resolving, etc. These are distinctly human endeavors.

■ When someone leaves your organization, tear up the job description. Let the new person create her own job thereby establishing greater commitment. This approach will also allow the new employee to build into the job more personally possessed existing skills thereby reducing the fear of the unknown.

■ Consider acting, not waiting until you have all the information. In a rapidly changing environment, by the time you think you have all the information, something new comes along. Reacting to the most current information available at the moment is a characteristic of success during change.

————

■ Suggest a team meeting with the agenda of gathering a complete list of the group's strengths. Spend the entire time allotted to the meeting verbalizing, listing and discussing individual and group strengths. This exercise will increase the team's confidence of their ability to succeed in the new environment. The first step toward developing a more cohesive team is to have individuals better understand each other, and a session devoted to strengths is designed to help that understanding occur.

Two other ways to facilitate individual understanding would be to:

1) Have each group member share a nonbusiness experience such as a pleasant childhood memory.

2) Have each group member complete this sentence. "You would understand me better if you knew that I...."

These exercises are not for all groups. It depends on how comfortable team members are with deepening relationships.

————

■ Recognize coworkers' new and innovative practices. Something must be in it for people to give maximum time and energy to the success of the change.

————

■ Encourage a reward structure that will help team members feel good about themselves in a changing environment. When people have a positive self-image about their ability to cope with change, even if they do not do as well in the new environment as they thought they would, they will not accept that defeat. Instead they will take on the challenge to try again. If they do well, they knew they would and they will maximize the opportunity.

If people have a negative self-image about their ability to succeed and they do indeed fail, they will back off and say, "I told you so!" If they succeed, they will say, "That was just dumb luck," and then level off in their performance to prove themselves correct and remain consistent with their self-image. Positive employee self-image significantly enhances the chances of success in the new environment.

――――

■ Be available to support coworkers. Ask how you can help. The list of how people want and need to be supported is as long as an NBA millionaire's arm. It is critical for a person to determine specifically how her team members wish to be supported. (Be careful not to take on others' responsibilities during this time. Your "friends" may attempt to off load what they consider excessive or scary work.)

――――

■ Develop a pros/cons lists for a clearer understanding of the actual effect of the change. This technique may cause some unstated concerns to surface. Then take time to eliminate as many cons as possible.

――――

■ Use vision/mission to draw others to the new environment rather than using goals/objectives to force a new environment. Generating excitement over the future creates a "want to" rather than a "have to." **People will follow a leader simply because of how much the leader cares**. Before people can muster up their full energy, they must have a reason. Provide your team with a good enough reason (vision/mission) and you will get their energy committed to organizational goals and objectives.

———

■ Put yourself into the shoes of the other people What is in it for them? Do they see the change as another application of the BOHICA (Bend Over; Here It Comes Again.) principle?

A study by the United States Chamber of Commerce determined that only nine percent of American workers saw themselves as a beneficiary of improvements in company productivity. (A similar study in Japan showed ninety-three percent.) **The easiest way for people to embrace a change is if the benefit to them Is personal, immediate and certain. The least enticing is when the benefit of the change is primarily organizational, delayed and a gamble.**

New technology workers may actually be in a position of creating new products, policies or procedures designed to eliminate their jobs. **What weight do workers give to the benefit versus the punishment of change?**

———

■ Unlearn controlling skills. One person does not really have control over another anyhow. When change is slow, one can exist with the illusion of control. When the pace of change accelerates, a participative style may be more appropriate. This style will allow the each person to be a contributing member to the change.

_____

■ When a major problem occurs during a period of change, and that may well happen, consider reducing the problem to its lowest common denominator. Karl Weick, an organization theorist, said, "**One reason we don't solve social problems is that we tend to define problems in such grand terms that we paralyze our ability to act**, i.e. drug problem, national debt, the bomb. Ironically people often cannot solve problems unless they think they aren't problems." **To be successful in the change business, take big problems and tear them into little problems that are solvable**. A person who is in trouble is one who will take little problems and roll them all together into one big unsolvable ball.

_____

■ Group exercise: Develop a list of potential beliefs concerning change. Ask group members to rate each belief on a scale of zero to ten. (Zero: I don't believe it at all. Ten: I live my life by it.) Obviously everyone will not believe exactly the same and with the same degree of passion. Then discuss the results. This discussion brings the internal game of change out into the open. You could also finish off the exercise by asking the participants to list five beliefs which, whether they hold them or not now, would make change easier. If necessary, refer them to Chapter Eight on how to rephrase self-talk.

_____

■ Keep organization simple. It is easier and faster to change a simple organization.

     -Simplify procedures.
     -Simplify communications.
     -Reward simplification.

-Eliminate organization charts.

———

■ Conduct a reality question and answer session with each concerned person in the group. Ask:

> -What are your negative beliefs about the change?
> -Do you really believe that will happen?
> -What is the best you can hope for from this
>   change?
> -What can you do to get what you want?
> -What can I or the organization do to help?

———

■ People usually go through a three-phased sequence in a new job:

> 1) Socialization — learning the job, the people, etc.
>
> 2) Innovation — doing the job, a highly productive
>   phase.
>
> 3) Adaptation — the job is routine. People may be-
>   come rigid. (Chronological age is not the
>   determining factor. Length on the job is.)

Recognize when you are in the adaptation stage. If you always have the answer to job questions, it may be time you moved on.

———

■ Once you and your group have determined what must be done to make the change work, be ready to change the plan you just made. Be flexible. Do not lock yourself into one set of behaviors. More effective behaviors may be waiting right around the corner.

———

■ Probe deeper when a coworker states only a rational reason for avoiding change. When the emotional reason is also uncovered both of you are on your way to a happy beginning. Do not attempt to negate the importance to the person of that emotional reason. Opening up on an emotional level takes courage. Whether you buy the reason or not, the important issue is, the individual does. And as Henry David Thoreau said, "When a dog is running towards you, whistle for him."

When we do not discuss the emotional issues, which are sure to be there, we dampen people's passion and caring about the success of the organization. **Consider the belief that all business is personal and people do care deeply about the organization and their coworkers**. Use that passion to implement change successfully.

———

■ Play the "So What" game with a person negatively concerned with change. Ask what he feels will happen as a result of the change. When an answer is given, ask, "So what?" He should take it one step further. Then you ask again, "So what?" Keep asking until the individual gets to the root cause. Example:

You: "What do you believe will happen when this change occurs?"

He: I can't do the new skills so I will screw up."

You: "So what?"

He: "If I screw up my salary might be reduced."

You: "So what?"

He: "If my salary were reduced and the company is down-sizing, I would probably be the first one to get fired."

You: "So what?"

He: "If I were fired, my family would leave me."

You: "So what?"

He: "No family, no money, I'd become a bum."

You: "So what?"

He: "If I were a bum, I'd probably become an alcoholic, drink Ripple wine from a brown paper bag and die of cirrhosis of the liver."

What is being said is if the change occurs, your coworker is going to die. No wonder he is concerned! Now would be the time for a reality check. What would really happen?

■ Ask for the tools and resources you will need to succeed in the new environment.

■ Support and encourage as a role model anyone in the group who approaches change in a positive, assertive manner, a person who will confront and test the limits. This is not always easy because **those folks who embrace and thrive on change may have broken the rules and cut the corners of systems management has put in place.**

■ Ask group members how they would change their jobs if they were "king." What would you change about your job if you could change your job? Work together to change whatever can be changed.

■ Take the scientific view to reducing the negative impact to change. Apply the Pareto Principle. Vilfredo Pareto, a 19th century economist, analyzed the distribution of wealth as between the "vital few" and the "trivial many." Pareto's idea is sometimes called the eighty/twenty rule. **Assume that eighty percent of the negative attitude toward change rests with only twenty percent of the change itself**. Concentrate on the twenty percent and work to reduce that twenty percent's impact. Time well spent!

■ Continue (or start) to network. Networking is the art of making and using contacts. With a broader range of contacts, both inside and outside the company, comes greater self-confidence and less concern with potential negative consequences of change.

■ Keep a careful watch on yourself and your coworkers for any behavioral signs of significant stress or burnout, signs such as: busy work, reduced personal energy, physical aches and pains, absenteeism, denial, illusions, sub-par performance, etc. Alvin Toffler states that a person has a limited biological capacity for change. Get help for yourself and/or your team members before any of you exceed that capacity. **While change provides growth, challenge and learning, it can also be debilitating when served in large chunks**. The same can also be said for too much stability.

■ A person must be aware of what kind of change is

occurring in order to apply the proper skills. If the change is the result of <u>more</u> work, then examples of the skills needed are faster decision making and quicker action while dealing with familiar issues. If the nature of change is <u>new</u> work, then look to learning, training, experimentation, etc.

■ Help develop a manager and employee shared sense of commitment to the organization's mission (substance). If the leader were to leave, and in an environment of high change, frequent transfers, promotions and out placements, this is quite likely, the group could function independently.

■ Be open to offering and receiving suggestions. A goal of organizations desiring to survive in an ever-changing environment should be to have all employees believe and behave as if the organization is their organization and to have the employees be willing to take personal responsibility for how it operates.

■ Help others visualize what the new environment will look like when it is running smoothly. Keep the word pictures positive. (Pygmalion Effect — positive expectations yield positive results.) Remember, the subconscious mind does not focus on the opposite of an idea. **Obstacles are those frightful things you see when you take your eyes off your vision.**

■ When the behaviors required in the changing environment are clearly defined, understood and accepted (This is called providing "feedfront" rather than the traditional, after-the-fact "feedback."), measure and reward the behaviors. **What gets measured and rewarded gets done**.

_____

■ If you feel there are some "unspoken concerns" lurking in the work unit, establish a procedure where coworkers can turn in unsigned 3 X 5 cards. Those issues can be openly and honestly addressed at the next group meeting.

_____

■ If in the design of the change, you have the option of too many activities in the new environment or too few (although both are undesirable), opt for the too few. To quote Drucker, **"The less an organization has to do to produce results, the better it does its job**." When designing the goals for those activities, shoot for high standards because only excellent performance of a job considered worthwhile, motivates.

_____

■ Ask for feedback as to how the change is going and what can be done to enhance its effect. **There is nothing as stimulating in an organization as everybody communicating with one another**. Don't be like that old limerick:

> I have come to this conclusion,
> It's one I've long supposed,
> The boss's door is open,
> It's his mind that's always closed.

Multi-directional communications (and your mind) must be kept open. Treat all feedback as a gift. Without it you are in the dark. As Lee Iacocca said, **"There are times when even the best manager feels like a little boy with a big dog waiting to see where the dog wants to go so he can take him there**." Listen to the dog.

_____

■ In the new environment you may find a skill required that you do not possess to the degree necessary. If one of your coworkers is of Olympic caliber in that skill, trade. You do one of her jobs while she does one of yours.

_____

■ Help develop a group problem-solving process. One suggested approach: have each group member state to the group, "The toughest problem I will have to face during this change will be...." Then let the rest of the group provide suggestions as to how that problem might be handled. This process provides individuals with more alternatives than they might have thought of on their own and creates a greater knowledge base for all group members, thereby reducing the individual and group learning curve.

_____

■ Consider getting input from outside of your work unit when contemplating change. Outsiders can see things you might be missing and add a new perspective. As the old saying goes, "I don't know who discovered water, but you can bet it wasn't a fish."

_____

■ Group meeting questions: "If we do not change; if we do not expand our comfort zone; if we do not try new ideas; if we do not become different than we are today; where do we see ourselves in two, three or five years?" Only when a person sees that doing things the old way or doing nothing is a greater risk than change, will the person voluntarily change.

_____

■ Make every effort in group discussions to get the group to focus on what they are <u>for</u> in the new environment, rather than to focus on what they are <u>against</u>. Too much energy is expended on what we do not want to see happen and since the subconscious mind does not focus on the opposite of an idea, we are generating no help from inside ourselves.

18

HOW TO CREATE AN ENVIRONMENT IN WHICH IT IS ACCEPTABLE TO FAIL

■ Tell everybody that it is acceptable to fail. (While chances are they may not believe you, it is a start.)

──────

■ Reward attempts, not just successful completions. If our parents had only rewarded our attempts at walking once we walked around the block, we would all still be prone on the living room carpet.

──────

■ Encourage open discussions on failures. When work unit members discuss their failures, other members of the team will learn without having to make the same mistakes themselves, thus maximizing the teaching power of the failure.

A word of caution: while there are benefits to "discussing" failure, rewarding failure itself may be another matter. This story provides a warning.

> A farmer sitting out on his back porch spotted a cat with a frog in its mouth. Feeling sorry for the frog, the farmer pried it out of the cat's jaws, and then taking pity on the cat, he poured a couple of drops of good sippin' whiskey into the cat's mouth. The cat left, but soon returned — with two frogs in its mouth.

We get more of what we reward.

———

■ Make it easy for others to try new ventures and conduct one-on-one discussions to determine what was learned.

———

■ Accept failure as a norm. It must be a norm in changing, evolving, restarting organizations. As the critic, Alexander Cogburn, said about A T & T after the breakup of the Bell System, "If you sawed the tail off of a kangaroo and told it to be a greyhound, the wretched thing would have problems too." Failure is inherent in change.

———

■ When failure occurs, and it will, be there to support coworkers how and when they need it. Recognize that every member of the work unit may need to be supported in a different manner. Find out how you can support each individual.

———

■ Create an open forum for discussions on failure as a concept. (Utilize Chapter Thirteen on failure as a starting point.)

- What are the team members' negative beliefs concerning failure?

- Conduct a reality check. What would really happen if a team member failed?

- What do the team members perceive would happen if they failed?

- How can group members reframe negative beliefs concerning failure? (See Chapter Ten on reframing beliefs.)

■ If you are a manager or team leader, call attention to any mistakes you make. No matter what the relationship between boss and subordinate, people are afraid of their bosses to some degree or another. Getting confirmation of what may already have been suspected, that the boss is not perfect, can strengthen the team bond.

■ Do not accept negative talk within the group concerning failure. Keep bringing the discussion back to "what have we learned."

■ Be an example for others on how to get "back on the horse" after failing.

■ Develop a short memory for your own failures (and those of others) and a long memory for successes.

■ Reduce the negative consequences attached to failure. As discussed in Chapter Thirteen, people do not fear failure as much as they fear the perceived consequences of failure (lack of approval from others, poor performance ratings, salary ramifications, etc.). Reduction of the perceived negative consequences will increase the desire to expand the horizons.

■ Request performance appraisals be rewritten to include a discussion on "Failure Ratio." It has been said our success does not rely as much on our IQ (Intelligence Quotient) as it does on our FQ (Failure Quotient).

■ Reduce your expectations concerning outcomes of

unfamiliar tasks.

_____

■ Parameters should be defined between employee and manager about what is acceptable and unacceptable failure. A balance must be struck, understood and agreed to, as to required productivity versus affordable mistakes. As Tevya, the lead character, in the musical, *The Fiddler on the Roof,* said, "**Life is like a fiddler on top of a roof, trying to scratch out a pleasant, simple tune, while simultaneously trying not to fall of the roof.**" Negotiate a balance.

_____

■ Admit you do not have all the answers, even if you think you do. That will encourage team participation in untried areas.

_____

■ Consider not referring to failures as "failures." It will aid in reframing if you refer to your handy Thesaurus and call your failures: mistakes, blunders, mishaps, botches, bungles, stumbles, slips, or depending on your level of sophistication, "boo-boos."

_____

■ Think carefully about quitting projects with which you are experiencing difficulty. Success may be just around the corner.

_____

■ When hiring a new employee, consider Peter Drucker's question. "**Do organizations tend to hire people who have the ability to do better rather than the courage to do differently?**"

_____

■ Encourage creativity. Creativity invites failure. If a person knows he is correct, there is no reason for creativity. As General William Scott said, **"Any fool can follow a rule. God gave him a brain to know when to break the rule."** Creativity often breaks rules.

———

■ Request the formal appraisal cycle be lengthened. Evaluating people over a longer period will provide a more conclusive indication of what was learned and the ultimate result of the failure.

———

■ Do not jump in to save the risk-takers. Let them learn from their experiences. One of the hardest tasks is watching but not commenting when somebody is doing something you know how to do, and they are doing it wrong.

———

■ Create a fun work environment. Laugh and take things only as seriously as they are. Don't ever cry more than a quarter's worth over a lost quarter. Remember **in the rat race, even when you win, you are still a rat**.

———

■ Promote multi-level training sessions so higher levels in the organization are seen for what they are, fallible human beings who make mistakes.

———

■ When preparing another's appraisal, discuss it with the person while the appraisal is still in a rough draft form. This technique will allow the employee to tell her side of the story rather than believing that whatever is said will not matter because the appraisal is already completed.

———

■ Ensure all team members understand the work unit mission. Many failures occur that are not seen by the person as a failure because the person thought he was doing what was supposed to be done.

––––––

■ Prove, by demonstrated behaviors, that you will be an effective buffer between someone who has made an error and the elements of upper management who are looking for the person's scalp.

––––––

■ Evaluate personal beliefs concerning your role and how that role relates to allowing coworkers to fail.

––––––

■ Develop the feeling of teamwork within the work group. Then when one member fails, others will be there to pick her up, thus minimizing the organizational productivity impact as well as the potential negative affect on the individual. **Punishment and intimidation push people away from teamwork and down Maslow's hierarchy of needs back to survival**.

––––––

■ Catch others doing things right and amplify their strengths. This focus will build the confidence needed to weather failure.

Providing positive feedback also aids the learning experience because people do not learn by forgetting. Concentrate on others' failures only if they become obstacles. To again quote Peter Drucker, "...**the only thing universal is incompetence**."

(Guard against creating a monster. Some people become so optimistic, they do not recognize failure. They totally disregard the negative experience, therefore do not learn, and they and the organization suffer.)

––––––

■ Focus on success; do not focus on avoiding failures at work. Focus on avoiding failure will only lead down the path of organizational mediocrity.

———

■ Become a "learner" in order to maximize each failure (as a learning experience) and reduce the number of unproductive failures.

———

■ Keep in mind that doing the right thing wrong is more important than doing wrong things right although neither is desirable.

———

■ Understand and be comfortable with the reality of primarily horizontal movement within today's rightsizing organizations. Workers with an eye toward climbing the ever diminishing corporate ladder will not be as willing to take a risk.

———

■ Continually emphasize the importance of the attainment of the work unit mission, not the process used to attain the mission (consistent with morals, ethics and the law). When watching mountain climbers making an ascent to the top, how often do you see them follow a straight line? The fact that their path may take them all over the mountain says more about the condition of the terrain (external events) than it does about the quality of the climbers (employees).

———

■ Use goal attainment meetings to focus on what has been accomplished and how the work group can do even better. Discourage sessions designed to beat up those not at 100 percent goal attainment. Goals, which in their purest sense are designed to draw the employee to a successful conclusion, are too often used to find fault with her performance and leave little or no room for failures.

■ Avoid comparisons between individual team members. The "Ha! ha! Eddie, you made a mistake and Mary didn't," approach shifts one's focus to evaluating his own performances compared to others not in comparison to the desired standard.

■ When discussing a failure with another, avoid putting it in the "past absolute." "*Every time* you turn in a report, it is incomplete and inaccurate." Instead try, "*Next time* you turn in the report, I am sure you will check to determine its completeness and its accuracy." This second approach allows the worker to visualize what future reports will look like rather than developing a focus on incomplete and inaccurate reports. This approach also maximizes the experience as a learning tool. **Punishment only tells people what not to do, but does not suggest what should be done**.

■ Encourage your organization to reduce those executive perks that separate the big guys from the little guys, i.e. perks like reserved parking spots, executive dining rooms, etc. These perks increase the dependency of the employee on the good will of the organization in order to, someday, also be a big guy. How could an employee accept failure with a key to the executive washroom at stake?

■ Practice the concept of "subsidiarity," which means never make a decision at a higher level that can be made at a lower level. This concept, combined with trust, will allow lower level employees to increase their knowledge (through potential failure) thereby producing a more knowledgeable and fulfilled worker. Also the boss can get on to doing other "boss things."

———

■ Recommend excluding new ventures when implementing compensation programs. Failure can then be truly viewed as a "learning experience."

19

HOW TO REDUCE FEAR OF LOSING SECURITY

■ Look for educational opportunities both inside and outside of the work environment. The mind-set of many workers in the larger corporations of the past may have been that everything needed to be known for job success would be taught by the organization. This "cradle to grave" educational philosophy certainly is not the mind-set of many of today's larger corporations.

Of course, even if workers score A's on all of their training, the self-confidence necessary to put the fear of loss of their security in its place is not guaranteed. Skill training is external and can be provided in and out of the organization, while self-confidence is internal and can only be provided by the individual. Each supports the other. **The prospect of losing job security does not negatively affect those with marketable skills and a self-sufficient attitude**.

———

■ Group exercise: Each individual answers, confidentially, on a 3 X 5 card if they intend to be in this organization in five years. Compiling the answers and then discussing with the group will generate different beliefs regarding security.

———

■ Distribute whatever current statistics are available from organizations such as the Bureau of Labor Statistics dealing with the reality of job security. Some interesting figures are: the number of employers the average American will work for over a lifetime, average job tenure in the United States, how many different careers the average person will be a part of, etc. (See Chapter Fourteen on Security.) These figures are often surprising to mid-career workers at major corporations.

———

■ Request a "rumor hot-line" to deal as openly and honestly as possible with each question concerning employee security. If you are a manager and do not have the answer or do not believe the answer you do have, go as far up the organization as needed. Get an answer that is satisfactory to the employee in doubt. Managers in some organizations may feel they are risking their own security by going around asking questions of upper level executives (a limiting belief in this case). Put yourself in upper management's place. Wouldn't you want to know what kind of rumors are going around which may be affecting employee productivity? Why would your executives be any different?

A major portion of a manager's job is to manage the environment so her people can effectively perform their tasks. When distractions such as rumors enter the workplace and disrupt the environment, the rumors must be managed.

When rumors of layoffs rear their ugly (and often accurate) heads, this is a particularly vulnerable time because many people become immobilized waiting for the other shoe to drop. This is not the position the organization wants its employees to be in when short-term productivity is critical. The manager must redouble his efforts to keep the group busy doing necessary projects, especially long-range projects to provide the belief of stability.

■ When dealing with group members, treat the subject of job security with humor. Do not address the potential loss of a secure position as the end of the world. (After all it does allow a person to sleep later in the morning.) Do not let coworkers give insecurity too much power over their ability to perform. Put the loss of a job in its proper perspective. As Larry Wilson, the founder of Wilson Learning Corporation and the Pecos River Learning Center, says, it is merely "inconvenient." The truth is employees were looking for a job when they found the one they have and they can always find another one. Losing a job or a specific position is not a tragedy, not the end of the world, just an inconvenience.

Human beings, due to the monumental amount of daily input to their belief systems, tune out everything not seen as a value or a threat. If the management treats a potential loss of security as a major threat, the employees are going to see it everywhere, thereby creating an unnecessary, detrimental effect on organizational and personal productivity.

■ Fight for your job or position by developing a "save this position" paper. This paper would address issues such as how the endangered position contributes to the bottom line of the organization and how the organization would be in more severe circumstances with the position eliminated than it would to fund the position. Also every job was originally designed to solve a problem the organization felt needed solving. What was that problem? Does the problem still exist and who will solve it if the position is cut? This is a productive exercise for everyone in the organization regardless of security issues.

———

■ Group exercise: Present this problem for each member to answer. "You have found yourself with no job, no money, no friends and in a strange town. Provide a detailed plan of what you would do." This scenario is, hopefully, worse than even your most pessimistic team member can conjure, but everyone will come up with a plan that is workable. By providing a plan, the exercise demonstrates that the person can still be in control. People can survive. The group needs to help each other focus on everything they have left, even after the major disaster, rather than focusing on everything they perceive is lost.

An alternate exercise, also designed to put the individual in the driver's seat, would be to ask each to list every perceivable negative outcome which has a probability of occurring should the job or current position be lost. Have individuals list after every Item what could be done to reduce the negative effect of that outcome.

Again this exercise shows that workers are not defenseless in the face of a cruel and uncaring outside world. Successful people rarely run out of options nor do they allow themselves to be locked into one pattern of thinking. You and your team members do not want to feel like the cartoon character, Ziggy, who turned down a car salesperson by saying, "No, I don't want to buy a car that has more options than I do!"

———

■ Ask your group members if they feel more secure, or less secure, today, at their current age, than they did at seven years of age. Ask those who answer that they are more secure in the present, to explain why. The explanation of the sources of their security will be of benefit to those not feeling that high degree of security. For those who felt more secure at seven years of age (Do not be surprised if this group is the majority.), initiate discussion on why this would be, considering at seven, they may only have had parents for security. Today many folks still have their parents but also a family of their own for support and to protect them. They also have more education, business and personal contacts, experiences, etc. The fact is that we should be more able to supply our own security today than we could at age seven. Why doesn't it seem so to everyone?

■ Recommend to all members of the work group that they prepare or update their résumés. Review each other's résumés and suggest each person provide an opinion on strengths seen. Also discuss what people may need to add to their personal résumés to be more saleable to another department or organization. If the organization perceives the mutual benefit of each employee being internally secure, reviewing résumés and practicing interviews may be a service the Personnel Department would consider providing.

■ Encourage group members who have played "fast and loose" with security to share their experiences, the good, bad and the ugly, with the rest of the group. Bring in outside guest speakers to shed some light on what life is like outside of your organization and to lend witness to the fact there are people living and thriving who have never even heard of your company!

Prepare a list of all of today's successful people who have been fired or "outplaced" in the past. This list will provide a balance to all of the negative thinking prevalent around the subject of security.

A good example of the power of dwelling on success rather than on failure would be using the hypothetical exercise of placing a 2 X 8 board on the ground and at one end placing a twenty dollar bill. Ask someone to walk the length of the board and retrieve the twenty. The same board is wedged between two buildings at about the tenth floor with a twenty dollar bill at the far end. Now ask that same person to walk the length of the board and retrieve the money. Might there be a difference between the way of walking (behaviors) under each circumstance. With the board on the ground, the participant would have a straight, quick and confident walk, while ten stories up, a slow, halting gait with arms flapping in the breeze would be evident, and yet the 2 X 8 surface is the same for both trips. The difference is, for the second trip, the walker was concentrating on the circumstance of failure rather than on the reward of success. The same is true with our coworkers. If they understand and concentrate on the success possible when individuals are self-sufficient and mobile, rather than concentrating on the potential negative circumstances of losing security, they would display more productive behaviors on the job.

———

■ Suggest individuals on your team question policies, test limits, and redraw organizational parameters. When workers discover they can test the extremes and can have a positive and real effect on the productivity of the organization and still survive, their concerns over security diminish. One definition of a rebel is someone who is several deviations off the cultural norm. Try to make being a rebel in your group, the "cultural norm."

────────

■ Review the Results Model from Chapter Six with the group and/or the individuals negatively affected by loss of security. The organization decides to eliminate a job or a position. That is an event. What are the positive and the negative beliefs which may be held concerning the event? Since the event has occurred and is not directly under the control of the employee, the choice of belief which is under the control of the employee becomes very important. Analyze the negative beliefs. Where did they come from? Are they appropriate in a dynamic business environment? (Ensure you get beyond the rational issues. This is the time for feelings.) If required, reframe the negative beliefs (Chapter Ten) and introduce positive beliefs into both self-talk and group talk. Might as well look at the event from its positive aspects, because it has happened!

────────

■ Ask the group to role play members of upper management. Provide the group with the kind of financial data and future projections that the "powers to be" may be using to determine the fate of the organization. Process the group through the question, "If you were in charge, knowing what you know, what would you do?"

While this exercise does not necessarily increase an employee's sense of security, it will give a better understanding of why there are "rumblings in the hallways." The employees may also come up with some innovative ways to save jobs and/or positions that the upper management may not have considered such as: retraining people, loaning employees temporarily to other firms, bringing work currently being done by vendors, consultants (gulp!) and suppliers back into the company, granting leave with some salary and medical benefits, etc. **All of us are smarter than one of us**. Any organization not utilizing this technique of employee input before a major restructuring is missing a bet.

■ Ask the question, "What would my dependents do if I were not able to provide the financial support I provide now?" Often the negative stress experienced over the potential loss of security comes from the beliefs that others would suffer immeasurably if the person were not caring for them. The purpose of this question is to generate reality. What really would happen to "dependents" (interesting term) without the present financial support?

■ Request to be moved often within the organization, i.e. build in a lack of security. Movement increases self-confidence in the ability to learn new skills, to interact with new people, to survive in a new work environment, to work for a new manager, etc. All of these experiences reduce concern over the elimination of a job or a position.

■ The work unit norm must become one of individual self-sufficiency. It must be understood that the employee and the organization will remain together as long as there is a mutual benefit. The organization cannot expect to hold on to 100 percent of its valued employees but must do what it can to benefit from them as long as they are employed. The employee cannot expect to remain employed if performance is unsatisfactory or if the organization cannot financially afford the employee's individual contribution. A mistake made by many individuals is to believe that they are working for someone else. **Both employee and organization must be ready to do without the other at a moment's notice**.

Interview for other jobs, both inside and outside of the organization, and encourage coworkers to do this also. Demonstrate that commitment must be to the quality, integrity and passion people bring to their work, not to any one job or position. Suggest cross training. Workers will have more to offer, and management will not be caught short of qualified personnel if the organization reduces its head count.

Organizations must invest in people's long-term growth through continuous education and development. At the same time, the organization should be shifting the limiting belief of some employees that they are employed for as long as they wish to be, to the more realistic belief that the employee does not control 100 percent of the employment "contract."

The employee must be ready to take care of himself when or if termination comes. This concept can be demonstrated using an exercise found in *The Magic of Conflict* by Thomas Crum. This experiential exercise is both educational and fun.

Ask one of your team to stand with feet shoulder-width apart, bent over at the waist and "walk out" with his hands until he is evenly supported by both hands and feet. Then ask another employee of about the same height and weight to stand perpendicular to the person doing the imitation of the "Golden Arches" and gently allow his body to lean over the bent back. The person in the down position is like a horse packing a dead soldier. Then you ask the question, "For whom do you think this position is most uncomfortable?" During the discussion it will become obvious that both parties are uncomfortable. The one on the bottom feels an obligation to keep the one on the top "secure." The one on the top does not have any control and if he wants to be "secure," the person on the bottom has to be kept happy. The metaphor of the organization feeling a responsibility to keep its employees "up" and the employees' dependence on the organization is clear.

Next ask the two volunteers to stand back to back with their shoulders touching slightly and gently lean into the other to feel the support. While the support each participant receives is evident, there is an understanding that each is not dependent on the other for security. If one person were to leave (either the employee or the organization), the form of the relationship would change, but the other would not be devastated.

————

■ Ask the total group to help its individual members become more secure in their own talents. Simple exercise: Group member, Craig, gets five minutes to be the center of attention. The remaining group members use that time to tell Craig what they think are the special talents he brings to the work environment and on what kinds of jobs these talents could be most effectively used. The group then concentrates its collective mind on each of the others in turn. It will quickly become obvious that every team member has definable talents which are also transferable to new jobs or positions.

■ Team members must watch their attitudes towards those coworkers who have been, or are going to be, released. The attitude should be one of helping the coworkers to optimize the experience. If the attitude is "Oh! poor them! Ain't that awful," it will be harder to keep the survivors with a positive, or at least neutral, view toward a lack of security.

■ Many people worry about being let go from their current positions and phrase that concern in these words, "I'll never be able to make this kind of money anywhere else!" Do a reality check. Is that true? Maybe not. List all the jobs that are available using the skills you now possess which could produce the money you feel is needed to survive. ("Needed to survive" is also a good subject for a reality check.)

This might also be a good time to analyze other reasons for fear of losing security. Money may not be the major issue. There are other concerns, i.e. the loss of interaction with peers, prestige, support from coworkers, intellectual stimulation, pride of the family and community, etc. How could these needs be met somewhere else?

■ An interesting point to discuss! Many people worry about losing a job or a position they really do not want. **The truth is that many people are afraid of losing a job they did not want in the first place and they do not even like very well now.** A Gallup survey of 1,350 people determined that forty-one percent consciously chose their jobs or careers; eighteen percent got started through chance circumstances; twelve percent took the only job available and the rest were influenced by friends or relatives. About half said that job stress affects their health, personal relationships or their ability to do their jobs. Nearly one third expect to change jobs within the next three years and sixty-five percent said given a chance to start over they would try to get more information about career options. And these are the jobs some folks are worried about losing!!

Following is a list of questions you may wish to ask which might put potential job loss into perspective. The first five questions are from Warren Bennis in his book, *Leaders*. He uses these as a five point exercise designed to help people decide if they want to remain in their present jobs:

— Do you find meaning in your work?
— Is the job teaching you anything that still interests you?
— Are you and your coworkers aligned behind a common
    goal?
— Is your work fun?
— To what extent are your personal goals "attuned" to
    those of the organization?

A couple of other interesting questions are:

— If you had no knowledge of what you have done or are
    doing for a living, what would you be doing now?
— If money were not an issue, what would you be doing
    now?

If the answer to either of these questions is different from your current occupation, what is the big concern over the potential of not having that job anymore?

Humans are the only organisms in nature who can voluntarily change and yet we fight it — especially when it comes to job changes. Tom Robbins in his book, *Even Cowgirls Get the Blues,* has one of his characters go with the feeling — he calls in well. The technique goes like this: You get the boss on the line and say, "Listen, I've been sick ever since I started working here, but today I am well and I won't be in any more."

———

■ On the top of most lists of rational concerns over potential loss of security is money. To assure you are giving this aspect all it deserves, and no more, a suggested exercise would be to list all current assets and liabilities, then develop a plan on how to manage, given the current financial condition as a base, for six, twelve, and twenty-four months. If that becomes tough to answer, try the question this way, "If you did know how to make a go of it, what would be your plan?" As strange as that approach sounds, it allows a person to address the problem from a different perspective. Absorbing the reality, whatever it may be, and creating a plan puts you in control.

———

■ If you are open to activities such as visualization, an exercise would be to visualize what a positive future would look like without your current job or position:

What would you be doing?

What must you do now to make this positive future a reality?

This is similar to using the "tombstone" approach to personal goal-setting. If you have gone to that "great employee picnic in the sky," how would you want your tombstone to read and what are you doing today to make it happen?

This could be an effective group activity also.

———

■ Utilize the "Alien" exercise discussed in Chapter Eight on Self-Talk. As a group, provide the self-talk In which the alien would need to engage to be stressed over a potential loss of security. Then discuss the fact we were not born with this fear. We are born with only two basic fears: fear of height and fear of loud noises. Since some people now fear losing security, that fear must have been learned, and **anything learned can be unlearned**. Then begin reframing through positive self-talk.

———

■ Keep catching people doing things right. This approach builds the self-confidence necessary in an unsure business environment. Since the first humans evolved over a million years ago, we spent ninety-nine percent of our time as predators. It is not always easy to catch people doing things right. We are used to catching things to eat them.

———

■ In a group discussion on security, open with this question as a conversation starter:

— How much security would you really want and how could you go about getting that degree of security for yourself?

Other general statements that could be used to kick off a discussion on security:

— When elderly people are asked what they most regret about their lives, it is most often the things they did not do.
— At some point employees will "max-out," i.e. reach their

highest level in either the corporate structure or growth potential from their current job. These employees then may seek out "losing" security because the pain of "plateauing" is greater than the pain of loss of security.

— "A fair day's work for a fair day's pay" will keep a person employed as long as she wishes. This old chestnut is not always true today. Highly productive workers are being summarily let go.

— Security is knowing what tomorrow will bring. Boredom is knowing what the day after tomorrow will bring.

— Children look at their parents and see lives that revolve around four events, the end of the work week, vacation, retirement and death.

— I will never be really secure as long I am in business to help other people accomplish their goals. The only real security is when I am in business to accomplish my own goals.

— If my main goal is security, I will always act with caution and in a dynamic organization that can only survive by taking risks, my termination could become a self-fulfilling prophecy.

— Fortune 500 industrial companies have dropped 3.2 million positions in the '80s and according to some studies, corporate America is still twenty-five per cent over-staffed. Peter Drucker says, **"There is no excuse for a business to have more than six layers of management."**

What does your organization look like?

—— ——

■ Recognize there are three stages people go through before accepting their own self-sufficiency:

— Bitterness: regret they are not getting the security they feel they need from others and they may never get it.
— Resentment: anger they are not getting the desired security.
— Forgiveness: pardon for themselves, bosses, families, etc., for not providing the security for them that was theirs alone to provide.

Understanding at what stage you and your coworkers may be will help you guide yourself and others to the next higher level.

———

■ Develop a personal purpose. That purpose can then direct you toward the kind of occupation to which you will be willing to devote maximum time and energy. (That occupation may or may not be the one you are currently in.) Questions used in our workshops to get at personal purpose are:

— What should I do (given my education, family finances, background, etc.)?
— What do I want to do?
— Why am I here?
— What do I have to contribute that will make a difference?
— What do I value?
— In what do I believe?
— Given the above, what seems to be my personal purpose?
— How can I experience my purpose, in my personal and work life?

Once a purpose has been defined, the expertise to accomplish it will soon follow.

———

■ Be available to help some of your more ambitious coworkers narrow down a long list of options. If individuals keep "all their options open," they may become immobilized with option shock which can lead to inaction, low energy, depression and despair. (See the Tactical Strategy Plan in Chapter Twenty-One.)

———

■ Read books which discuss the future of business in the coming decade. This information will provide a head start on the knowledge needed to be successful in the coming years. (See the Suggested Reading section.)

———

■ Recognize the potential "Survivor Syndrome" that may be displayed by those who are left after a downsizing. There may be the feeling that the reduction in force was unnecessary or that their former coworkers were given a raw deal. Survivors are experiencing more work for the same money, if they are lucky, with less chance for promotion. They may also be waiting for their turn to be "outplaced" or for the entire organization to fold.

A poll conducted by Right Associates, an outplacement firm, determined seventy-four percent of senior management at recently downsized companies said their workers had low morale, feared future cutbacks and distrusted management.

The survivors are actually going down the triangle on Maslow's hierarchy of needs. The organization requires its core of employees to work well as a team, have good self-images and even, if possible, be self-actualized; yet many workers are reverting to safety issues. This is a tense time in any evolving organization and one requiring understanding, patience and, above all, truth.

■ Effective communications with those undergoing the self-imposed trauma induced by a potential loss of security are essential. If the dialogue is to do any good, it must deal with feelings — virgin territory to some.

Here is an activity to try: Come to an agreement prior to a discussion (either one-to-one or in a group) that all parties will follow this procedure: Party A will not state her views until party A has restated what party B has said and party B agrees that party A has "got it." When it is party B's turn to speak, he will do the same with party A. This approach ensures that each person has listened to the other, and by repeating party A's words, party B may get new insight.

20

HOW TO INCREASE SELF-ESTEEM

■ A manager's responsibility is to define and communicate the work unit mission using group input. (This is who we are; this is what we do and this is what we believe in.) In order to increase its effectiveness, the mission must be one the members feel has meaning, substance and is worthy of their time. Being committed to some worthy endeavor comes first and when that commitment exists, a person can always develop the necessary expertise. **With an important enough "why," a person can always figure out "how."**

Working daily to accomplish a mission that has personal meaning will go a long way toward helping individuals feel good about themselves. To maximize this energy, ensure each individual, regardless of level, has a clear understanding of how his specific job function aids the organization in the accomplishment of its mission.

―――――

■ Use "home grown" talent to aid in the growth of other team members. Establish positions of mentors, trainers or in-house consultants. Performing in these positions of leadership may help enhance self-esteem. (A word of caution, be sure to get the person's permission before granting them this "honor." Additional work of this type is not everybody's cup of tea.)

―――――

■ Employ the synergy of the group to help each member.

Conduct the following exercise at one of your group meetings:

Each person takes one minute to complete this statement, "The strengths I bring to the team are...." They then have the full sixty seconds to verbalize what they feel their strengths to be. (If they stop halfway through their allotted time, there will be thirty seconds of silence. Each person gets the full time.) When the individual is finished telling her strengths, the rest of the group has three minutes to finish this statement, "The strengths we see you bringing to the team are...." Again, a full three minutes are to be used. The individual and the group stated strengths are then to be captured in some form. The session could be audio or video recorded. Each participant would get a personal tape to play back. Or a recorder could be appointed to write what is said, and each would receive a written document containing all stated strengths. In those dark hours when team members might not feel the confidence needed to perform even the simplest task, they could take out the results of this session and reinforce that they are, in fact, pretty darn good. Since the conscious mind does not hold two simultaneous, contradicting beliefs, people do not feel bad about themselves at the same time they are feeling good about themselves.

When you introduce this exercise, the team may look at you as if you have taken leave of your senses. (It is a look I know since this exercise is conducted in some of our workshops.) But when they leave the session, they will be walking about a foot off the ground. Martin Luther King Jr. called it the **"Drum Major Instinct," that desire each of us has to stand out and to be special**. This exercise is highly recommended to help individuals feel like drum majors. Imagine an entire session where all that is mentioned are strengths. What a powerful and productive experience!

———

■ Miscellaneous ego builders — delegate authority to make decisions to levels or individuals not previously having that authority. This may be a natural fallout from downsizing and empowerment, yet it proves a positive side effect for the ego of those so entrusted.

Egos are also fed when people have access to "inside" information, choose flexible working hours, make their own job titles and evaluate their managers at the formal appraisal process. A manager might also consider putting employees on a team with a revolving leadership position and/or asking group members' advice. (After all who knows more about the job than the person doing the job?) Transferring an employee to a high profile position and/or asking a worker to attend meetings with upper levels raises employee self-esteem. Also asking team members to make important presentations or to fill in as team leader adds to individual self-worth. Providing a dual-ladder system, if possible, that would allow for a professional and a managerial career track and permit more people to be promoted can enhance self-esteem.

———

■ Consider a community service leave for yourself or recommend such a leave to team members. These are leaves which involve loaning people to work for community organizations like United Way or to teach courses in local colleges or universities. Taking on these leadership roles will enhance self-confidence and provide a more experienced team member. Sabbaticals will provide some of the same individual and group benefits.

———

■ People feel better about themselves on the inside if they believe they look good on the outside. Keeping a healthy state of mind is easier if that mind is in a healthy body. Request installation of fitness facilities within your organization or if that is not practical, join an outside facility. Maybe your organization could pay part of the membership fee.

———

■ Set high, meaningful and worthwhile goals. It means more to a person's self-respect to be held accountable and to achieve a "stretch" goal than to achieve a goal expending little or no effort. Ensure group goals are tied to the mission of the work unit and the relationship is recognized by team members. **To attain goals day after day without seeing a relation to the big picture can create a condition of drudgery**.

Use goal attainment as a mark of achievement so people feel better about themselves and their abilities. As influential as the goal setting process can be in increasing self-esteem, the goal setting process can be as influential in decreasing self-esteem if the lack of attainment of a stretch goal is used as a tool to beat people over the head. **How is the goal-setting process perceived in your organization?**

———

■ Encourage initiative. Ask others what should be done and how to do it. When this input is requested, use as many suggestions as possible. Conducting brainstorming sessions when appropriate helps draw out coworkers' ideas and gives a tangible reinforcement that their contributions are valuable.

———

■ Match a person's abilities with the job requirements and make the tools available to promote the highest chance of worker success.

———

■ Employees find difficulty thinking well of themselves if the boss is treating the employees as if they have some form of communicable disease. This limiting mind-set is demonstrated by the boss throwing every imaginable organizational block in the way of interpersonal communication with her team, for example: the boss stays in the office with the door closed hours on end; appointments must be made through the boss's secretary; communication by memo is the norm; phone calls and employee initiated correspondence go unanswered. **Employees will gauge the manager's priorities based upon where the manager spends her most valuable commodity — time**. Does the boss spend time working with the people or pumping out reports from the safety of her office? What is more important, reports or people? Managers who interact with their people, help their people feel good about themselves. Interacting makes good business sense, another solid benefit of "Management by Wandering Around."

Managers need also to watch they are not a part of an organization attempting to get the most out of its employees while keeping employee rewards to the minimum required to keep the employee on the payroll. The employee will feel used and undervalued, and will get back at the organization by giving the minimum effort required to stay employed. A lose/lose situation all around!

———

■ Management should insist that employees take all of the vacation time due them. A more well-balanced life may help employees feel better about themselves because they can do a more effective job of meeting commitments in other aspects of their world. Convincing an employee to take vacation is not always easy. The culture in many organizations in the United States is one of "Anybody who does not hold over vacation from one year to the next is a wimp, not to mention a poor team player." This thinking is a cultural belief issue because in many European countries an employee is judged as being important by how much vacation he takes, rather than how much is not taken. (A sample of the average number of vacation days in different countries: West Germany, thirty; Italy, twenty-five; Great Britain, twenty-four; France and Spain, twenty-one; and the United States, twelve).

Vacation time can be optimized by taking the days in larger chunks of at least a week at a time. Taking a day here and a day there never really allows an employee mentally to leave the job. Also the other employees know he is only going to be gone for a short time so they leave all the work. The vacationer returns to more work than before.

———

■ Consider requesting someone be brought in from the outside to be a "sounding board" for coworkers going through self-doubts precipitated by change, i.e. someone with the expertise and/or experience to help employees overcome feelings of personal inadequacies. When a person is plagued with doubts over her abilities to perform effectively during change, it is very difficult for that individual to address these doubts directly to her manager. Many employees have a deep-seated feeling, born out of years of experience, that if they expose their "weaknesses" to their managers, nothing may get done to help them and that they will see them as "developmental needs" in the next performance appraisal.

People must be able to get help for their self-doubt without fear of reprisal. Using someone from the outside may also help the individuals get "inside" of themselves deeply enough to get at the root of their perceived limitations. Self-examination is not always easy as illustrated in the following story.

> A man was down on his hands and knees on his front lawn obviously searching for something in the grass. His neighbor came over and asked what he was looking for. The man said he was looking for his keys. The neighbor, being a helpful sort, got down on his hands and knees to help. After a few futile minutes the neighbor asked, "Where did you lose them?" The man said, "In the house." The befuddled neighbor questioned, "Then why are we looking out here on the lawn?" The man replied, "Because it's dark in the house!"

Contained in this light-hearted story is a serious message. **Looking outside in the light for the source of perceived limitations is easier, but it is a good bet the answer is inside, in the dark**.

———

■ Explain the facts. Often workers have been led to believe that their worth to the organization will be shown through promotion. (Of course nobody ever says exactly that, but why do so many people believe it that way?) When promotions stop, as the people hit their plateaus, does that mean the person's worth has "plateaued" also? This plateau point in a person's professional life can be tough on the ego and will require some open and honest communications between the employee and management.

As a part of preparation for a meeting with someone discouraged due to a lack of upward advancement, consider reading Judith M. Bardwick's book, *The Plateauing Trap.* This book contains all the statistics and common sense a person needs to comprehend the reality that there are more potential "promotees" than there are positions to which to promote them. This BGO (Blinding Glimpse of the Obvious) is the reason promotions end long before retirement for almost everybody. The book also contains suggestions as to what a person might do to help those in this situation feel good about themselves.

■ Do not let a meeting end without asking an opinion about the subject being discussed from each team member. Every opinion has some modicum of value. Find it and thank each for the contribution. All of us feel important when our views are considered.

■ Be careful when listening to someone else's ideas. Coming up with a "better" idea is easier when someone suggests something to you first. You have the benefit of their idea plus your thoughts on their idea which combined may be a better idea than the original. That process may make you look smart, but is a win/lose for the other person.

■ Create an environment of learning. Encourage group members to ask questions, to attend training both inside and outside of the company, to read, to listen to and/or to watch educational tapes. People must take personal responsibility for overcoming perceived limitations. Management's responsibility is to set the learning climate. Tom Peters gets serious about this subject when he says, **"It's immoral to be a manager in business and not let a person maximize his or her potential."**

———

■ Ensure when you provide problem-solving feedback to others you talk about measurable and observable behaviors. If you tell people they are not flexible, not creative enough or not properly market focused (None of which are behaviors.), they tend to take the criticism personally. Even worse they do not have the slightest idea of how to fix the problem, which only contributes to a decrease in self-confidence.

Deal with behaviors, a set of measurable and observable motions which can be changed. ("The compilation of sales figures you did for this report is not up to your usual standards. Next time I am sure you will include the eastern region's forecast.") People feel a greater sense of control. They know those behaviors are not them, just something they do or do not do, which can be changed.

While "catching people doing something right" (positive feedback) is important to increase their self-images, it is not always possible. To reduce the ego damage, stick with what they did or did not do, and stay away from criticizing them as persons.

Feedback, letting the individual know how he is doing, is an important factor in dealing with a person's self-confidence. Utilize problem-solving feedback (negative) sparingly compared with reinforcing (positive) feedback; but do use it. Problem-solving feedback lends credibility to the reinforcing feedback and, after all, bad breath is better than no breath at all!

———

■ Provide maximum behavioral autonomy to team members consistent with their work maturity. Consider the Managerial Freedom Scale developed by William Oncken Jr.:

1) Wait until being told.
2) Ask what to do.
3) Recommend, then act.
4) Act, but advise at once.
5) Act on your own, routine reporting only.

The team's responsibility is to move its members from one to five, thereby creating a more proactive and self-confident team.

———

■ Try this exercise to enhance your own strength awareness. When you are with a large group of people in a train station, an airport or a crowded street, take time to be aware of every person and find something good to say about each. Perhaps you will notice someone's straight posture, another's well-coordinated clothes, or someone else's friendly smile. The purpose of this exercise is to help develop more awareness of what is really out in the world. The same exercise can be used in your work unit. When you look for the strengths, you will see strengths; when you see them, tell your coworkers.

———

■ Since perceived limitations, which create self-doubt, exist because the limitations are believed and not the reverse, help your coworkers perform a reality check. People get down on themselves for a variety of reasons. For example, they cannot do everything perfectly (everyday, garden-variety perfectionists) or somebody does not like them (a basic need to be loved). Moving people past this type of thinking is difficult because all you can use is logic and they are dealing from a position of emotion, but try it anyway.

Engage the person in a discussion in which you bring up points such as:

— Is it possible to do everything perfectly?

— The plus side of perfectionist thinking is when something is done, it is done well. The down side is nothing will be attempted that might not be done perfectly which severely limits learning experiences.

— Trying to be sure everybody likes you is an interesting pastime, considering there are now close to six billion people playing in that game with you.

Also watch for a dangerous thought-pattern which happens when a person believes the past is at fault for what he is today and the past cannot be changed. This individual is then doomed to stay the way he is for the rest of his natural life. When you recognize a coworker falling into this trap of "no-win" thinking either through the types of limiting beliefs just mentioned or more obvious personal put-downs such as "I can't...," "I never...," "I should be able to...," or I am...," call attention to it, and help the person reframe.

Try the "RID" technique. <u>R</u>ecognize when a person is engaging in limiting thinking. <u>I</u>dentify what is being said or done so the individual is aware. <u>D</u>iscuss and give the person some other input so she can reframe.

Is there any rational reason people should be nicer to others than they are to themselves? If what is being said concerning perceived limitations is in opposition with reality, people can get real confused and a "learning disability" will occur. When that situation presents itself, it must be brought to the surface and discussed. Surprisingly, the hardest part of the RID process is for the individual to recognize when she is engaging in limited thinking. Here are a couple of fun examples which may help people recognize what negatives they are saying:

a) One organization bought a supply of little, metal, finger-operated clickers to make a clicking sound every time anyone in the group said anything that sounded like either an individual or group put down. The person who recognized the put down clicked the clicker to call attention to that word, phrase or action which created or advertised the perceived limitation. For awhile, until people recognized what they were doing to themselves, it sounded like crickets during mating season throughout the entire organization.

b) A variation on this approach, used by another company, was to use squirt guns to remind people they might be their own worst enemies.

———

■ Practice your best listening skills. It is hard to make people feel more important than to have somebody really listen to them.

Think about it. **When was the last time somebody really listened to you**? In workshops only a smattering of hands go up in response to that question. When asked to explain how it felt to be listened to, the words were much like the words a person might use to describe a religious experience.

Following are some basics to keep in mind when listening to your team members:

Care about what is being said. This makes all other skills of effective listening easier to apply.

Ask questions to clarify your understanding of what is being said. Clarification is important because there are 500,000 words in the English language. The average person knows 5,000 and the 500 words most used have 14,000 different meanings.

Take notes if appropriate.

Repeat the information to ensure understanding. Sum up what was said to get mutual agreement that the message sent is the message being received.

———

■ Greet people by name. It is hard to find a simpler gesture to please another and build his self-esteem.

■ If you are a manager, change how you view the relationship between you and your team. Scrap phrases like: "my subordinate," "Patricia, who works for me," "my direct reports," etc. Consider using: "associates," "partners," "team members" or "people with whom I work." These terms are closer to the truth and they help people feel better about the importance of their role in the accomplishment of the team mission.

A manager insisting on being called by a title like Dr. or requiring members of his/her team to use Mr., Mrs. or Miss is saying more about his/her own limitations than the employee's position.

■ When people feel they are lacking something they need to think better of themselves, ask this question of them: "If you could wake up tomorrow and have gained any one new ability, what would it be?" When you receive the answer, gently explain that the odds are not good that they will wake up tomorrow with that new ability, but right now they can begin work on what they need. Help them develop an action plan. An action plan format you may wish to use: (See Chapter Twenty-One.)

— State the desired results.

— Objective (How much of what by when?)

— Action Steps (What behaviors have to be done?)

— Feedback Devices (How will they know if they are succeeding?)

— Rewards (What is in it for them? How will they feel?)

— Support (Where will they go for help when they need it?)

People must really believe they have the power to initiate major reductions in their perceived limitations. To make this point, discuss the basic concept of hypnosis. Why are people able to accomplish behaviors under hypnosis they say they "cannot" do? The person has the ability. The conscious mind is just passing judgment on the ability to perform. When the conscious mind is temporarily out of the picture, the activity can be performed. Therefore **people have the ability to improve themselves; they just need to believe in their ability**.

Studies have shown that twelve percent of people's success lies in their abilities and eighty-eight percent with their attitude; **an attitude can be changed this very moment**. Suggest starting with a very simple question, "Am I doing my best?"

———

■ Advanced self-doubt can manifest itself in depression. Watch for signs. According to the American Psychiatric Association, a person suffers from major depression when he shows at least five of the following symptoms within a two week period:

— irregular sleeping patterns.

— irregular eating habits.

— recurrent thoughts of suicide or death.

— depressed mood.*

— loss of interest or pleasure in daily activities.*

— significant weight loss or gain.

— agitated or retarded movements.

— feelings of worthlessness or guilt.

— lack of concentration.

(*Either must be at least one of the symptoms.)

Group members should be alert for these signs. They should be ready to address the issue tactfully with the affected person and to support his efforts to regain emotional equilibrium.

———

■ Perceived personal limitations are relative. When a person says she is not assertive enough, a question could be asked, "Compared to whom, Charlie Brown or Attila the Hun?" People may have expectations of what they should be and too little understanding of how far they have come. You can add input as to where you see the person on the continuum from zero skill to 100 percent skill. Discuss any discrepancy between your perception of placement on the continuum and hers. Encourage her to develop a plan to move further towards 100 percent. Most people do not have as far to go as they might think.

———

■ Asking what person, living or dead, team members would most want to be like will kick off discussions designed to surface major causes of personal frustration. (Problems may exist if someone wants to be like Paul Newman, but is like Alfred E.)

Have each participant list, in column A, what is lacking for him to be like the chosen hero. In column B ask those participating to list where those ideas (beliefs) began. In column C, have them reframe the beliefs. They should then design an action plan to make up any perceived limitations.

People need to understand they do not have to be like their heroes to be successful. They just have to be the best they can be. An old quotation states, **"Rabbi Zusya said that on the day of judgment, God would ask him, not why he had not been Moses, but why he had not been Zusya."**

———

■ Treat each team member as an individual. Everybody brings something different to the workplace. Remember, there are strengths everybody has. There are strengths some people have and then there are strengths, due to personal uniqueness, only an individual has.

———

■ Ask group members who may be short of self-confidence to list five current or hypothetical beliefs which could help them feel better about themselves. Then refer those people to Chapter Ten on reframing. The following may also help people when reframing their limiting beliefs:

A study was conducted in which scientists placed a barracuda and a mackerel in the same tank. This arrangement seemed fair to the barracuda who loved to eat mackerel but did not seem so fair to the mackerel who did not want to be eaten by anything. Who said life is fair? What the scientists did not tell the barracuda was they put a heavy glass partition between the two fish. The barracuda, seeing lunch on the other side of the tank, took off at top speed and ran head on into the glass partition. Mr. Barracuda's hunger overrode his fish brain, so he repeated the "banging the glass" scenario a few more times. Then he decided he was not so hungry after all. Once he stopped going for the mackerel, those crafty scientists removed the glass partition. The mackerel then swam right in front of the barracuda and the barracuda got a headache just watching it. The barracuda did not go after the mackerel, obviously, because the barracuda knew what he could or could not do! **So often in people's lives, they are living in the present with limitations that were internalized in another time.** Time to reevaluate and reframe.

———

■ Group exercise: have each group member describe every other group member, in a sentence or two, on a separate 3 X 5 card. Pass out the cards to the persons they were written about and ask people to stack their cards in piles marked positive, neutral and negative. This exercise accomplishes two objectives: first, people see how they are perceived by others and second, individuals get a good indication of their self-image by seeing in which pile they place the cards.

If they see themselves as highly intelligent, cards that do not mention intelligence will probably go on the neutral to negative pile. If they do not see themselves as attractive and they are described as such, they may place that card on the neutral pile because they are not sure what to do with it. This is not an exercise to be discussed very deeply after completion because where the people place their cards should be confidential. Each individual will have something to think about regarding self-image, and how each is perceived by others.

———

■ Nelson Burton, a professional bowler, when asked about the secret of his success, said that he always had, from childhood on, confidence in his ability to be a championship-caliber bowler. This positive mind-set began when he started bowling. His scores were always good because as he would roll the ball slowly down the alley, his parents would move the pins in front of the ball. They made sure little Nelson did well and added points not only to his bowling score but also to his self-confidence. Anything you can do to "move the pins" for your coworkers will pay off significantly in the long run.

Group exercise: Have members of your group team with a partner. Each person will spend the next five to ten minutes explaining in detail to her partner about a very successful outcome achieved, either business or personal. Explaining exactly what was done and telling the skills and talents she brought to the success will give a big "pat on the back" to the teller. During the process she should attempt to recapture the feelings experienced when succeeding. When things are not going so well, time should be taken to recapture those confident feelings and to remember, "I am O.K.!"

———

■ Do not tolerate group members putting themselves down. It weakens the individuals and the team. For a demonstration of this concept, try this exercise at a group meeting: Ask for a volunteer. (Big, macho guys are the best.) Ask him to make a fist and extend his right arm in front of his body, angled down and to the left. (Left handed people, reverse the process.) Ask for a second volunteer. A person smaller than volunteer number one will best demonstrate the process. Ask volunteer two to try to push volunteer one's arm down. Volunteer one should attempt to resist. (You will have no problem with this part from big, macho guys.) You will get the results you expect.

Next ask volunteer one to relax, close his eyes and repeat at least ten times aloud, "I am a weak and unworthy person." It is important he really gets into this "being unworthy" business. Now repeat the arm pushing part of the exercise and ask both volunteers if they noticed any difference. This demonstrates the mind/body connection that results in less than satisfactory behaviors from those individuals who do not think of themselves as "worthy."

To conclude the exercise, have volunteer one relax again, close his eyes and enthusiastically say aloud, ten times, "I am a strong and worthy person." Put volunteer two to work again pushing on volunteer one's arm and get both volunteers' reactions to this attempt. Discuss the differences with the entire group.

———

■ Managers should consider the company's formal appraisal process to be an excellent way to highlight employees' strengths. The performance appraisal will provide a structured process to discuss strengths and developmental needs (only if the developmental needs create an obstacle to achieving required results), and to develop an action plan to improve performance. This review process is not generally thought of as the premier event of the year for either the employee or the manager. Why not?

The review process may have a bad reputation because many managers conduct a session of this kind only once every twelve months. **When a manager spends only one hour discussing what he has been avoiding discussing (and the employee has been avoiding asking about) for approximately 250 working days, it is bound to be an uncomfortable meeting**.

The information contained on a formal performance appraisal should never come as a surprise to the one being appraised. (Anyone who has been on either end of that situation knows this to be true.) Use daily contacts with employees to let them know how they are doing. Formalize the process at least quarterly to emphasize strengths and the progress being made to reduce the developmental needs. Also discuss what is expected of the manager and the employee in the future.

———

■ An employee/manager relationship should begin with mutual trust. Mutual trust helps increase the self-esteem of both parties. (See discussion on mutual trust in Chapter Twelve.)

———

■ Watch how your team members react to "failure." Are they surprised they did not do as well as anticipated? Are they preparing to get it right next time, or are they giving up? Their reaction is a good indication of self-image in that area. Coworker support may be needed to increase the person's self-confidence for the good of the individual and the organization.

Team members could lessen the negative personal effect on a coworker regarding any perceived failure by asking the individual to analyze the experience and extract everything she did right. In most cases the person will be surprised to find more was right than wrong. This exercise will not only serve as a learning experience but also as a confidence builder.

———

■ As with everything in life, we do what we do because there is more perceived pleasure than pain. Therefore, there must be something in it for individuals to feel good about themselves and there also must be something in it for people to be down on themselves. You will want to do everything in your power not to reward a coworker's misplaced self-doubt through additional attention. Utilize attention to reward examples of the person's self-confidence.

———

■ Be a role model, but not of someone who has all the answers or all strengths and skills. (They probably wouldn't buy that anyway!) Be a model of a person who knows what her skills and strengths are and is not shy about using them.

———

■ Strive to keep the work atmosphere light-hearted. Nobody is going to get out of this life alive, except possibly Shirley MacLaine. Keep perceived limitations in proper perspective. Do not let individuals in the group get too serious over their perceived limitations. After all, how bad can things be when even a broken clock is right twice a day?

How many talents does any individual really need? Consider there are only four primary colors, eight base notes in music and twenty-six letters in the alphabet and the musicians, artists and writers are doing all right.

If the group is getting too serious, ask them to engage in a technique from Zen Buddhism called the "Monkey Meditation." For five minutes they all assume the most absurd positions they can achieve, laughing at themselves and others. Only a real uptight group will stay serious after a session like that.

We have all heard the expression, "Don't sweat the small stuff." Here is one explanation of what "small stuff" is. Maybe you can use it for people who get too serious. "**Birth, big stuff; death, big stuff; everything between, little stuff.**"

■ Two chart exercises to determine individual talents:

1) Quadrant Chart

- Draw a vertical line and label the top Skills - Easy to Do. Write at the line bottom Skills - Hard to Do.

- Draw a horizontal line through the center of the vertical line. On the left side, label Skills - Hard to Learn. On the right end of the horizontal line, write Skills - Easy to Learn.

- Now the participant should place the skills he now has in the appropriate quadrant.

Society values those skills that fall into the "Skills - Hard to Do" and "Skills - Hard to Learn" quadrant. A person's real talents fall into the quadrant marked "Skills - Easy to Do" and "Skills - Easy to Learn." Those are the talents a person has been given to enhance society.

2) Column Chart

- Divide a piece of paper into three columns. Head column number one, <u>What am I good at?</u>; Column two, <u>What do I find easy to do?</u>; Column three, <u>What is one of my special abilities?</u> Answer each of those questions at least six times. Consider the answers to see what theme emerges.

The obvious objective of each of these exercises is to get individuals to do self-analysis to recognize all they have going for themselves. Few people are ever as limited as they think they are.

———

■ If the situation arises where the manager must initiate "punishment" of some type, care should be taken. The purpose of any punitive measures is to correct a problem so the negative results will not occur again. **Punishment primarily designed to hurt the employee and secondarily to correct the problem is an example of position power by the manager.** "I'm the boss; I am bigger than you, therefore I win."

The real focus toward solving a problem is to attempt to accomplish a positive result without either the manager or the employee feeling less capable. Also punishment itself has some basic down sides:

— People get used to punishment after awhile.

225

— Punishment may keep people from doing anything, even the right things. (Remember Mark Twain's story of the cat on the hot stove lid.)

— Productive energy is wasted by people coming up with excuses.

— The worker/manager relationship is adversely affected.

— Punishment could lead to "fight or flight."

An interesting example of the potential negative effects of punishment is told in the story of the little boy and the pickle jar.

> Once upon a time there was a little boy who "spit" in the pickle jar. (That is not the way the story was heard, but that is the way it will be told.) That night at dinner his father went to reach for a pickle. The little boy began to feel guilty. So he told his father about spitting in the jar. The father "laid hand" upon the child and sent him to his room where the little boy was to stay until reaching the age of puberty. This punishment did not stop the child from ever again spitting in the pickle jar, but it stopped him forever from telling his father.

■ You may wish to suggest this interesting technique to people who are having difficulty putting negative self-talk into perspective. Ask them, "Where, in your body, does your self-talk seem to come from?" Most typical answer is, "From my head." Then suggest they have the self-talk originate from some other body part, e.g. a big toe. Having your big toe say you are no good at adapting to change takes on a whole new significance. Another technique is to self-talk with the voice of a favorite cartoon character —— "Tha...tha....tha.....that's all folks!"

21

TACTICAL STRATEGY PLAN: HOW NOT TO
EAT THE ELEPHANT WHOLE

So now what? You are the proud possessor of more than seventy pages containing 175 "how tos" designed to create a change environment. Some of the suggestions will quickly be eliminated because they are not appropriate for your particular situation, individual team members or work group in total. What about the remaining activities? How do you decide what to do and in which order?

The following Tactical Strategy Plan (TSP) is designed to answer the "what" and "which order" questions.

<u>Steps to implement the Tactical Strategy Plan (examples on pages 232 and 233)</u>:

1) Determine which of the roadblocks (Pain of Change; Fear of Failure; Fear of Loss of Security; Self-Doubt) to effective change you wish to address to reduce negative impact on team/individual productivity. (For the TSP example, we will use Fear of Loss of Security.)

2) Select ten (10) activities you feel would be most useful in reducing negative impact. (For demonstration purposes, we will choose the first ten "how tos" from Chapter Nineteen, "How to Reduce Fears of Losing Security.") Only choosing activities from the roadblock being worked on is not necessary. For example, you may be working on overcoming the roadblock of fear of loss of security (Chapter

Nineteen) for yourself or one of your team members, but if you find an appropriate activity listed under any other chapter in this section, use it.

After becoming more familiar with the TSP, you will see that the process is equally effective using more or lo00 than ten items. For this learning exercise (and since the forms in this book are designed for ten), please select ten.

3) In order to determine which of the ten items would be most effective in accomplishing the desired result, this step will be used to compare each activity to the other nine activities. This is done by deciding which of the two compared activities (if you could only do one of them) would be most critical to achieving positive results.

For example, using Chapter Nineteen, "How to Reduce Fear of Losing Security," is it more important for you to:

- Provide educational opportunities?(1)
                    OR
- Conduct a group 3 x 5 card exercise?(2)

If you think in your particular environment, it is more important to provide educational opportunities (1), pick number one and place a 1 in the comparison box for activity #1 versus activity #2. (See the Relative Importance Grid on page 232 example.) (When selecting which activity is to be done, select the more important activity. Importance is the criterion.) Then move on to the next comparison that of activity #1 versus activity #3.

To reduce team members' fears of loss of security, is it

more important to:

- Provide educational opportunities?(1)

OR

- Distribute current statistics?(3)

   If you feel it is more important to distribute current statistics (3) than to provide educational opportunities (1), enter 3 in the comparison box for activity #1 versus activity #3, if not enter 1. When finished comparing activity #1 to every other activity, then move on to activity #2 and compare 2 to 3; 2 to 4; 2 to 5, etc. Continue comparing activities 3 through 10. When this step of the TSP is completed, every activity will have been compared to every other activity. Each activity will have been rated as to its relative importance in overcoming the selected roadblock. (A word of caution: A football coach once told me, "Don't think. It weakens the attack." When comparing two activities, go with what your gut tells you. Do not try to overthink each comparison or you will be retired before you decide what to do.)

   4) Each of the chosen activities has now been given relative importance. To determine which activities have been chosen as most important, total all the appearances of each of the numbers you have written within the grid. Total how often 1 was chosen, how often 2 was chosen, etc. Since there are forty-five boxes in the grid, the total should be 45. If you do not get 45, retotal. Every time a number appears, count it. For example 6 may appear in either the vertical or the horizontal "6" columns.

   5) How well is each of the activities being performed right

now? This step is to rate, from 1 through 10, your current performance of each activity. If you have done nothing on the activity, rate the accomplishment on that activity a "0." If the activity is already accomplished, give it a "10." If some progress has been made, maybe a "5" or a "6."

6) We are now ready to plot the results on the Priority Profile (page 233). Each activity will have an importance rating (step 4) and a performance rating (step 5) In our example, number 1 has an importance rating of 7 and a performance rating of 3, so number one will be placed at the intersection of 7 and 3 on the profile.

TACTICAL STRATEGY PLAN WORKSHEET

RELATIVE IMPORTANCE GRID

	2	3	4	5	6	7	8	9	10
1. Provide Ed. oppty.	1	1	1	1	6	1	1	9	1
2. Group Exercise (3x5)		3	4	2	6	7	2	9	10
3. Distribute Current stats.			4	3	6	7	8	9	10
4. Develop rumor Hotline				4	6	4	4	9	4
5. Treat subject with humor					6	7	5	9	10
6. "Save the Position" paper						6	6	9	6
7. "No job - No money" exercise							7	9	10
8. Question security, today vs age seen								9	10
9. Group members update resumes									9
10. Experience Sharing									

IMPORTANCE RATING
(Total all appearances of this number within the grid. Total = 45)

1. 7
2. 2
3. 2
4. 6
5. 1
6. 8
7. 4
8. 1
9. 9
10. 5

TOTAL 45

EXISTING PERFORMANCE
(How well is the listed activity being performed today? 0 = No activity 10 - Accomplished)

1. 3
2. 0
3. 2
4. 8
5. 9
6. 1
7. 0
8. 10
9. 2
10. 6

TACTICAL STRATEGY PLAN
WORKSHEET

PRIORITY PROFILE

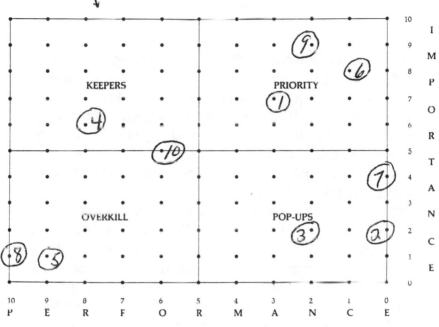

POP-UPS	Low Importance. / Low Performance
	(Time and energy currently spent on these activities will produce minimal results.)
OVERKILL	Low Importance. / High Performance
	(Consider diverting time and energy devoted to these activites to priority items.)
KEEPERS	High Importance. / High Performance.
	(Appropriate use of current time and energy to these items.)
PRIORITY	High Importance. / Low Performance
	(Best use of current available time and energy to generate desired results.)

ANALYZING THE TSP

Analyze the findings of the Tactical Strategy Plan. Any activity falling into the lower right quadrant of the profile (Pop-Ups) is an activity that is currently not too important in accomplishing the desired result. That is acceptable because you are not doing it very well anyway. How about activities in the lower left quadrant (Overkill)? Those activities are activities felt to be of minor importance in accomplishing results but you are "doing the hell" out of them. Upper left are those activities (Keepers) which are important and you are doing them well. The activities falling into the upper right are those activities (Priorities) relatively important in accomplishing results and currently not being done as well as they could be. **If a person has limited time and wishes to spend that time most effectively, performing the activities appearing in the Priority Quadrant would produce the best return.** Blank forms, including a Tactical Strategy Action Plan for implementing your chosen activity, are included for your use on pages 236-238.

●●●

Suggestion: After about three to six months, run another TSP using the same ten activities. What do you think will happen?

Shifts will occur. If you were working on the priority items, they will shift to the left into Keepers and those in the lower right may "pop-up" to Priority, those in Overkill may shift to Pop-ups.

The TSP is a dynamic way to rank a "too long" list of activities, for example "The Fifty-Two." **Use the Tactical Strategy Plan format for prioritizing both business and personal lists. The TSP is also an excellent team activity for objective setting**.

TACTICAL
STRATEGY PLAN
WORKSHEET

RELATIVE IMPORTANCE GRID

	2	3	4	5	6	7	8	9	10
1.									
2.									
3.									
4.									
5.									
6.									
7.									
8.									
9.									
10.									

IMPORTANCE RATING
(Total all appearances of
this number within the
grid. Total = 45)

1. _____   6. _____
2. _____   7. _____
3. _____   8. _____
4. _____   9. _____
5. _____   10. _____
   TOTAL _____

EXISTING PERFORMANCE
(How well is the listed activity
being performed today?
0 = No activity
10 - Accomplished)

1. _____   6. _____
2. _____   7. _____
3. _____   8. _____
4. _____   9. _____
5. _____   10. _____

236

TACTICAL STRATEGY PLAN
WORKSHEET

PRIORITY PROFILE

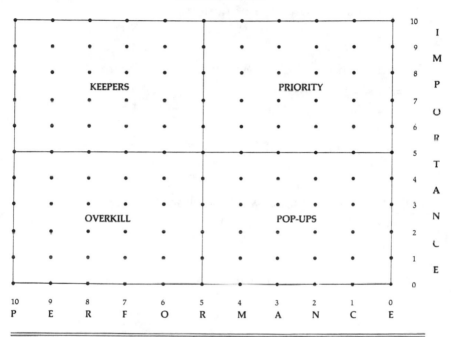

POP-UPS
Low Importance. / Low Performance
(Time and energy currently spent on these activities will produce minimal results.)

OVERKILL
Low Importance. / High Performance
(Consider diverting time and energy devoted to these activites to priority items.)

KEEPERS
High Importance. / High Performance.
(Appropriate use of current time and energy to these items.)

PRIORITY
High Importance. / Low Performance
(Best use of current available time and energy to generate desired results.)

TACTICAL STRATEGY PLAN
WORKSHEET

Plan of Action

State desired result and develop a strategy to implement.
Be specific in all categories.

Desired Result_____

Objective (How much of what by when?):

Action Steps (What do I have to do?):

Feedback Devices (How will I know if I am succeeding?):

Rewards (What is in it for me? How will I feel?):

Support (Where will I go for help when I need it?):

CONCLUSION: FROM THE INSIDE OUT

You say your organization has merged, acquired, expanded, split, rightsized, consolidated, centralized, decentralized and restarted five times since you began reading this book. Welcome to the future. **Change is a given. Change is a way of life**. We can play "Woe Is Me" twenty-four hours a day or we take control and make change work for us. **The only constant in organizational change is the individual, regardless of what the evolving structure looks like**. Organizational change is all of us, the managers and the employees. How we, individually, relate to the change will spell the difference between success or failure of the new endeavor.

●●●

The introduction to *From the Inside Out* gave us fifty-two needs that more than 200 people actively involved in business today felt will be required for success in a changing environment. The fact that a person might take the rest of his time on earth to master all of "The Fifty-Two" is acceptable, because due to individual work situations that Herculean task should not be necessary. By using the Tactical Strategy Plan format detailed in the previous chapter, a person will be able to determine which of "The Fifty-Two" would be most beneficial for use in his or her specific situation.

●●●

Allow me to get less analytical than the TSP and give my gut level view of the needs of a worker in a changing environment.

If I could wish one ability for the person focused on succeeding in an ever-changing game, one ability that would provide the most leverage toward success, I would choose —— self-sufficiency. Self-sufficiency is the ability to stand alone, to take care of self, to know what is wanted and to go after it. Self-sufficiency is also to be "whole" without the necessity of anything else on this earth to be complete. **A self-sufficient person may desire certain affiliations with organizations or relationships with others, but does not need them in order to validate personal existence.** That degree of self-sufficiency would be a major ingredient in allowing a person to create (and not only to survive, but to flourish in) a culture of change.

Consider the importance of self-sufficiency when reviewing "The Fifty-Two." Is a person with a high degree of self-sufficiency inclined to be more flexible, innovative, and creative; to be more open to change, more enthusiastic, and more fulfilled; to be more of a learner and empowerer; to be more giving and worthy of trust?

Even those needs that require more specific "skills" (providing employee career development, planning capabilities, project management skills, etc.) are more evident in a self-sufficient person. A self-sufficient person would be more inclined to take personal responsibility to get what she needs to succeed, rather than to wait around for someone or something else to provide for her.

Would a self-sufficient person be inclined to implement more of the "how tos" listed in Section Three? Would a self-sufficient person allow himself to be motivated by fear generated by organizational dependence? Would a self-sufficient person be less tense, less frustrated, less stressed and therefore more productive because he has taken control?

Self-sufficiency starts on the inside as what we choose to believe about our ability to succeed without being unrealistically dependent on organizational or personal relationships. Self-sufficiency reduces the negative impact of the roadblocks to change. People who can "stand alone," choose to view change as a chance to learn and grow and to see failure as a learning experience necessary for increasing success. They consider themselves as the source of their own security and internalize what they have become as "pretty darn good."

●●●

Organizations need continually and positively to adapt to the environment they serve. The environment changes and, for survival, so must the organization. Since the organization is a group of individuals banded together as a group of teams formed to accomplish a specific purpose, **if the organization is to make significant change, so must the individuals who make it up**.

To produce effective, productive, long-term change, each employee at every level must question the validity of the status quo, test the established limits, push at existing organizational paradigms, and be "willing to walk." That will not happen without a strong sense of self.

From the Inside Out

●●●

Change occurs from the inside out, from the inside of each of us through what we choose to believe. Then change is manifested on the outside through what we choose to do about what is believed. An organization also changes from the inside out. The inside is every individual who makes up the organization. When individuals reach "critical employee mass," the organization will then change on the outside in relationship to its stakeholders and the environment. All begins with us, the people, and it begins on the inside whenever we are ready........ Ready?

SUGGESTED READING

A Company of One: The Power of Independence in the Workplace, Tom Payne, Performance Press of Albuquerque.

Aftershock, Harry Woodward & Steve Buchholtz, John Wiley & Sons.

All I Really Need To Know I Learned in Kindergarten, Robert Fulghum, Villard Books.

American Business and the Quick Fix, Michael McGill, Holt Company.

Augustine's Law, Norman R. Augustine, Penguin Books.

Changing the Game - The New Way To Sell, Larry Wilson & Hersch Wilson, Simon & Schuster.

Choices, Shad Helmstetter, Simon & Schuster.

Coaching for Improved Work Performance, Ferdinand F. Fournies, Van Nostrand Reinhold Company.

Do What You Love, the Money Will Follow, Marsha Sinetar, Paulist Press.

Fifth Discipline, Peter Senge, Doubleday Currency.

Future Shock, Alvin Toffler, Bantam Books.

Illusions, Richard Bach, Dell Publishing.

Suggested Reading

Imagineering for Health, Serge King, Theosophical Publishing House.

Leaders, Warren Bennis & Bert Nanus, Harper & Row.

Leadership Is an Art, Max DePree, Doubleday.

Man's Search for Meaning, Viktor Frankel, Simon & Schuster.

Megatrends 2000, John Naisbett & Patricia Auburdene, William Morrow & Company.

Peak Performers, Charles Garfield, Avon Books.

Powers of the Mind, Adam Smith, Summit Books.

Pulling Your Own Strings, Dr. Wayne Dyer, Avon Books.

Reinventing the Corporation, John Naisbett & Patricia Auburdene, Warner Books.

Service America, Karl Albrecht & Ron Zemke, Dow Jones-Irwin.

Seven Habits of Highly Effective People, Stephen Covey, Simon & Schuster.

Strategies 2000, Carolyn Corbin, Eakin Printing.

Starting with the People, Daniel Yankelovich & Sidney Harman, Houghton-Mifflin.

The Addictive Organization, Anne Schaff & Diane Fassel, Harper Row.

Suggested Reading

The Empowered Manager, Peter Block, Jossey Bass Publishing.

The Inner Game of Golf, W. Timothy Gallwey, Random House.

The Magic of Conflict, Thomas E. Crum, Simon & Schuster.

The Plateauing Trap, Judith Bardwick, American Management Association.

The Power of Purpose, Richard J. Leider, Ballantine Books.

The Relaxation Response, Dr. Herbert Benson, Avon Books.

The Renewal Factor, Robert Waterman, Bantam Books.

The Transformational Leader, Noel Tichy & Mary Ann Devanna, John Wiley & Sons.

The Unheard Cry for Meaning, Viktor Frankl, Simon & Schuster.

Trigger Points, Michael Kami, McGraw-Hill.

Thriving on Chaos, Tom Peters, Harper & Row.

Winning the Innovation Game, Denis Waitley & Robert Tucker, Berkley Publishing.

You Will See It When You Believe It, Dr. Wayne Dyer, William Morrow & Company.

INDEX

INDEX

INDEX

INDEX

NOTES

NOTES

NOTES

NOTES

NOTES

NOTES